God's Help for Parents with Adult Children

Hope and Healing for Extended Family Relationships

Gregory B Grinstead

Copyright

God's Help for Parents with Adult Children
Hope and Healing for Extended Family Relationships

Copyright by Gregory B Grinstead

All Rights Reserved. This includes the right to reproduce any portion of this book in any form.

First Printing January 2015

Books > Christian > Parenting Adult Children
Books > Christian > Extended Family Relationships
Books > Parenting > Young Adults

ISBN-13: 978-1511851404

ISBN-10: 1511851406

Contents

PART ONE

PART TWO

CONTENTS

Dedication

This book is dedicated to my four kids.

Dawniel the Peacemaker
Andrea the Firebrand
Nicole the Kind
David the Strong

It has been my Privilege and my Blessing to be your father.

Parenting you has been a wonderful,
Adventurous stewardship of love.

May you have the courage to start many things.
May you have the strength to endure the journey.
May you have the grace to finish well.

A Note to the Reader

This book was written in two parts. Part I explores the experiences of most parents when their children become adults. Part II has been written with stand-alone chapters. Each chapter reflects what I might say to you if you came to me asking for help with your family relationships. So for example, if you came to me and asked, "When should I help financially?" (Chapter 12's title) this is some of the things that I would say to you. As a friend talking to a friend, I try to address some very complicated issues.

In every neighborhood, in every community there are hundreds of adults who have really, really bad relationships with their newly independent children. For those who are not fully cut off and continue in relationship with their adult children, the relationships are strained, broken or just bad. These parents are wounded and confused. Many suffer not understanding what went wrong.

I will always remember the pain on the face of one of my friends, one Sunday morning when he said, "She doesn't relate to us anymore. She has cut us off and is living in the basement of her husband's parent's house. We don't talk." He stated this with an attitude of hopelessness and confusion. He was a loving father, husband and good Christian. He was really hurting.

Each story in this book is a real story about real people struggling to love and relate to their adult children. I take these real life situations and apply more than a two dimensional view of God's love and wisdom to the situations that many parents encounter. There are probably many paths to the healing and strengthening of your relationships.

May God use this book to comfort, encourage and instruct you. May you have the best relationship that you can have with your adult children.

Introduction

My first child was born 2 months premature. Four pounds at birth Dawniel almost didn't make it. From that first day, when we brought Dawniel home from the hospital, our actions were dictated by one thing. Our first concern was the welfare of our children. Until David moved out in 2005, every decision had that thought attached to it. Dawniel was a Bicentennial baby in 1976. David graduated in 2005. For twenty-nine years, my wife Michelle and I carried the wonderful responsibility for our four children.

We geographically moved to have our children go to better schools. When I went into ministry full time, our thoughts were for our children's welfare. We moved out of the suburbs of Southern California to the foothills of the Tehachapi Mountains because it was a better place to raise our children.

All decisions were filtered through the prism of our God given responsibility as parents. The first question we asked was, "Will this be good for our kids?" We sacrificed many things to have Michelle be a stay-at-home mom.

There are hundreds of books written to help parents succeed with children from birth to the late teens, but there are few written to the parents of adult children. Throughout history grandparents and great grandparents have been a blessing in the extended family unit. But in the last decades there has been an increasing devaluing of older parents and grandparents in our culture. This disconnection of the generations has led to the deterioration of the extended family.

When I was a young father, I mistakenly thought that my continuing education as a parent had stopped once my kids left home, got married and started their own families. My continuing position as dad was a kind of foggy, unknown area. I was not aware that the role would evolve and challenge me as much as the earlier years had.

God's Help for Parents with Adult Children

No matter how good a parent you have been the process of adjusting to having adult children can be very challenging and sometimes even traumatizing. The better at parenting that you have been in the elementary and teen years, the harder the transition may be. And that can come as quite a shock.

I always assumed that Michelle and my sacrifices and our intentional parenting would pay off with their respect and closeness in my later years. But adult relationships, especially between relatives, can be complicated and are not automatically good. This mistaken concept that adult relationships are automatically good between you and your adult children can lead to many regrets.

This book continues your education as a parent into this new season. I am asking you to take the same attitude that you had when you began parenting your small children. The process of change requires a focused approach to learning.

There is one new problem. The rules have changed. If your child gets mad at you, they don't run into their room and slam the door. They just remove you as a friend on Facebook, or they don't return your voice mails.

I do not agree with the unbiblical thinking that the older generations should be put out to pasture. Nor do I agree with the present practice of my generation of being mainly concerned with their happiness and fulfilling their bucket list, now that the kids are gone.

You have a valuable place in your children's lives.

God bless you as you read this book. May it help you have the best relationship that you can have with your children.

And God bless our children.

1

Why Christian Parents May Have More Problems with Their Adult Children

A Christian Friend's daughter was so excited when Proposition 8 was struck down by the Courts. The California voters had determined that marriage was to be defined as a union between one man and one woman, by an overwhelming majority. But the courts decided that this could not be done and my friend's daughter "Celebrated" on her Facebook page. She is a Christian and married to a minister. She did not share her parent's belief system.

Her belief system has been formed by the Bible, the Church, Doctor Oz and NBC News. Her friends on Facebook have shared their naïve understanding of justice and fairness. She is in the process of either growing in wisdom from life experiences or turning from the path that her parents had hoped she would walk.

Your child's generation has developed their value system and world view from many different sources. Instead of understanding the true experiences of history and the teachings of the Bible, they have been exposed to "truth" from people who have had a hidden agenda. Your child like their peers may now approach moral issues with the question, "What feels right." In the case of Proposition 8, it just felt right to redefine marriage.

For every really good idea that molded their view of life, they were exposed to 10 really foolish ideas. Your kids have lived through a time of cultural disruption. Foolish concepts are repeated as unquestioned truths. The latest "good" idea must be right. It sounds so right.

Good, sincere Christian parents have a well-defined belief system. They usually apply this system in a rigid way to their life-styles. The way they vote; pay their taxes and relate to their neighbors is guided by this Bible based morality. In contrast their adult children are in a process of finding what they believe. This process causes a clash that can be enlightening or destructive. This process can last for years as your child listens to the latest TED talk or educates themselves on subjects that they were taught in Sunday School.

This chapter has a few simple (but not over simplified) Biblical principles that can guide you through this process with your child. In some ways this whole book is about how you can navigate this path without making things worse. I have found that my lack of preparation for this season of parenting has, at times, left me baffled at what to do. Learning the seven principles of this chapter is the beginning of you being prepared to help guide the process of this clash of belief systems.

Biblical Principle 1
Relationships Need Radical Help

"Behold, I am going to send you Elijah the prophet before the coming of the great and terrible day of the Lord. He will restore the hearts of the fathers to their children and the hearts of the children to their fathers, so that I will not come and smite the land with a curse." *The last verses of the Old Testament - Malachi 4:5-6 NASB*

The Old Testament ends with a promise and a warning. The Warning is about a curse that will come to our world when the relationship between adult children and their parents are broken. The Promise is that God is going to take unprecedented steps to restore those relationships.

I do not know God's timing of the "Great and Terrible Day of the Lord." This specific prophesy points toward a time on this Earth when parents and adult children will not have love for one another. Parents will become so offended or self-centered that their hearts will be turned away from their children. Adult children will be so deceived or self-absorbed that they will break all contact with their parents.

Why Christians Have More Problems

The 21st Century has brought us to a time as this. Although parents and their children have always had many difficulties, intact extended families were the norm. Throughout history parents and their adult children have had some type of continuing relationship. Either because of necessity or parent to child brain chemistry bonding families did not break into the smallest group possible.

We have now entered a time when in Western Civilization the norm is slowly shifting to families voluntarily choosing to isolate themselves from one another. We may be living in the time of the prophecy of Malachi 4.

Biblical Principle 2
Leave and Cleave

'For this reason a man shall leave his father and mother
and be joined to his wife, and the two shall become one flesh
Matthew 19:5 NASB

Jennifer was a girl in her early twenties who had just gotten married. Jennifer had always been the responsible child and had continued a good relationship with her parents as she went to college and graduated.

She laughed as she told the story of her mother calling less than 24 hours after her wedding just to tell her that the family had made a lot of extra food. "Would she like to come over for dinner?" I am not sure if her husband was invited. Because she had been so close to her mom and had been the "Good" child, her mother hadn't thought about anything changing. Her mother's attitude was she wasn't losing a daughter; she was just getting an extra bedroom.

It is wonderful to hear that a married child could laugh about their parents not understanding the "Leave" part of the above scripture.

The old saying, "We are not losing a son. We are gaining a daughter," is great to welcome a new person into the family but it isn't Biblically accurate. Weddings change things. A disconnection happens. But many parents put pressure upon their children to stay connected while the disconnection happens. I am not sure how they think that is supposed to happen.

God has a plan for your children. They are to disconnect – leave and then reconnect as different people. This process of growing up and becoming an adult, separate from parents is clear. But the process of how it is to happen is left undefined, for good reason.

I grew up in Iowa, where generation after generation of young men would get married and build a house on the "back 40 acres of the family farm" and continue to farm with their brothers and father. The process of disconnecting and reconnecting is different for each generation and each culture due to diverse circumstances and personalities.

But the fact is that, if your child follows God's plan, barring tragic circumstances, they will leave and grow up. That is the job that parents have been called to accomplish. Raise them to leave. So let them go the right way.

Biblical Principle 3
Grownups Are To Honor Their Parents

"Honor your father and your mother,
that your days may be prolonged... *Exodus 20:12 NASB*

Sandwiched between "honor the Sabbath day" and "you shall not murder" is the moral law that has a promise directly from God attached to it. Many times this commandment is taught to small children as the same as "Obey your parents." And of course we want to teach our children all of God's moral laws, but this commandment is directed toward adults.

If you have learned to honor your parents, it will be easier for your children to adjust to honoring you when they grow up. They might not obey you, but they are commanded to honor you. Since this is one of the original Ten Commandments, it is one of God's foundational instructions on the right way to live.

When your children choose to not follow God's instructions they are not living correctly. The time for you to model this behavior toward your parents is while your children are small. If you did not model this behavior then, start now. Ask God to teach you what it means to honor your parents, even if you don't like them. I have written a whole book about how, when and why to honor your parents. It is this books companion.

Biblical Principle 4
The 7th Thing the Lord Hates

These six things the Lord hates
Yes, seven *are* an abomination to Him:
one who sows discord among brethren.
Proverbs 6:16,19b NKJV

Jan had been a member of our church for many years. She had written a heart wrenching letter to her adopted father about things that had happened and why she felt the way she did. The letter was emotionally disturbing and could only be understood by her and maybe her father, although his agreement was not at all guaranteed.

I had encouraged her to write the letter and she had reluctantly agreed. It did make sense to at least try to address the obvious problems that no one seemed to want to talk about.

Months later, not really surprised, she learned that her father had given the letter to her sister and her sister had called relatives and read edited portions of the letter to anyone interested. Her sister had caused trouble throughout the family, spreading partial information. The seeds her sister planted continue to bear the fruit of division, discord, and painful breaks in the family's relationships.

The moral of this story is not, "Don't do what your counselor tells you." The moral is that family problems can motivate "good" people to do things that God hates. God hates the act of sowing seeds of discord, because those seeds grow into mature plants of hatred, division and deception.

When sides are drawn even unintentionally, people recruit others to be on their side. They break confidences; twist the truth to make themselves look better. Proclamations of disloyalty to one group tugs and pulls people apart. Others fearfully try to keep everyone together by sticking their fingers in their ears and humming to themselves. The emotional atmosphere becomes dark.

God would prefer us to be on the same side; His side. There are some things that we do not need to know. We should all have finely tuned "gossip detectors." When someone comes with information that they, "just want you to be aware of," sirens should sound. Just don't participate in the conversation. Stop the sowing process.

There is one encouraging note to the above story. Jan's relationship with her father did not get better and he died without reconciling. But years later, a relative told her that when her sister had called asking her if she wanted to hear the letter Jan had written her father, this relative said, "No." If only more of us would say, "No."

Biblical Principle 5
All Humanity Has Family Problems

Adam's son killed his brother.
Lot was seduced by his daughters.
Noah's son uncovered his nakedness.
Esau's birthright was stolen by Jacob.
Joseph's envious brothers sold him into slavery.
David's son usurped the kingdom.

One reason we can believe in the truthfulness of the Old Testament is that no one would make up a story like this, about themselves. When most people tell stories about themselves, they are usually the hero of the story. The Old Testament and New Testament reveal the brokenness of sinful humanity and there is no place like home for that brokenness to be manifested.

The stories of the Bible do not teach some "Cult-like" idea that if we only do "Step 1, Step 2 …" we will be shielded from the suffering of men. The Apostle Paul established the First Century Church on this principle.

> They returned … to Antioch, strengthening the souls of the
> disciples, encouraging them to continue in the faith,
> and *saying*, "**Through many tribulations** we must enter the
> kingdom of God." *Acts 14:21b-22 NASB (emphasis added)*

Let us all be encouraged that the Bible shows us that every human is touched by the problems of other humans, especially in their family. It is clear that living your life in agreement with God leads to many blessings and even miracles; but escaping other people's pain is not promised to anyone. The pain we feel when touched by those the closest to us is the most intense. When things are going great, rejoice and be thankful. Jesus put it this way.

> Therefore do not worry about tomorrow, for tomorrow will
> worry about its own things. Sufficient for the day *is* its own
> trouble. *Matthew 6:34 NKJV*

Biblical Principle 6
Moral Clarity Brings Division

> "Do not think that I came to bring peace on earth. I did not
> come to bring peace but a sword. For I have come to 'set a
> man against his father, a daughter against her mother, and a
> daughter-in-law against her mother-in-law'
> *Matthew 10:34-35 NASB*

God would like us to all be in unity and live in harmony with one another. That unity should be centered in God. Having moral clarity will make your closer to some and will cause division with others. Unfortunately that division and tension may be with those of your own household.

Biblical Principle 7
Winning People without Compromise

Your goal is to have the best relationship that you can have with your adult children. But that relationship should not be one based in a moral fog. Your core values should not change because your adult children do not hold the same view. The Apostle Paul learned how to fit into most circumstances without compromise. He stated:

> For though I am free from all men, I have made myself a slave to all, so that I may win more. To the Jews I became as a Jew, so that I might win Jews; to those who are under the Law, as under the Law though not being myself under the Law, so that I might win those who are under the Law; to those who are without law, as without law, though not being without the law of God but under the law of Christ, so that I might win those who are without law. *I Corinthians 9:19-21*

Although the Apostle Paul had learned to not alienate those around him, he was beaten up and excluded from fellowship. God can help you not alienate your son or daughter and still not compromise when disagreements over moral issues arise. Parents of teenagers learn to choose their battles and not major on the minors when discussing teenage behavior. Expand that concept to your adult children.

There will be times that those in your own family will challenge why you believe what you believe. Most of Christianity's values can easily exist in harmony with nonbelievers. Few who want a moral society would reject the majority of Christian morality. Atheists don't want to be lied to; don't want their houses robbed; don't want the innocent harmed...

Why Christians Have More Problems

When your 40 year old daughter or 15 year old granddaughter comes to you asking why you believe what you believe be prepared.

> Be intellectually honest
> Be gracious and open to discussion
> Be respectful and non-dogmatic
> Be clear about the Bible says
> Be bold with a kind attitude.

The most important attitude of heart is to be full of love for the one who questions or challenges your belief. It is a good thing that they are talking about these things with you. Don't draw back in fear. Don't become defensive. Thank God the conversation is happening and take Paul's advice above. Win them with more than, "That's what the Bible says."

Other Reasons Addressed Later In This Book

This chapter did not explore the many other reasons Christian Parents may have more problems with their adult children. This book tackles some of the other reasons, such as;

1. Many Christians are broken and troubled individuals.
2. There are spiritual assignments against those who make a difference in this world - Christian and non-Christian.
3. Many Christian parents are sincere but not equipped to discuss cultural issues in an in depth way. Sunday morning teachings are full of simplistic and sometimes foolish ideas.
4. Christian parents have fallen into a trap of thinking that their job stops when their children go to college.

2

Your Job Is Done

A New Job Has Just Begun

There is an appointed time for everything… Eccl. 3:1

Your job is done." The thought came to me without warning. "Your job, of molding and making your children into good people – people living with correct values is done. Your job as a parent is done."

As a pastor, I had always taught that a parent's job is to work themselves out of a job. If done right, a good parent will raise children that do not need their parents. But when it happens to you, it can be a shock. Decades of my life had formed my internal identity. I was a parent. I was a responsible parent. I was a sacrificing parent. Now what was I? My job of parent of minor children had come to an end.

My wife and I defined our jobs as parents as having two main goals.

    1. To keep our minor children alive; to keep them emotionally and physically healthy.
    2. To guide, correct and instruct them toward being good people with correct Christian values.

A lot of energy went into goal number one. Providing shelter, food, clothing had taken many resources and a lot of time. Admonitions to not run into the street had given way to praying for them as they drove in the rain. Family vacations filled with driving down the highway, learning multiplication tables had morphed into Saturday afternoons spent in much too loud gymnasiums. So much time had gone into goal number one.

Goal number two above was guided by our Christian beliefs which came from only one book, the Bible. Trying to mold our children into good people seemed to be a never ending job of repeating loving instruction, wise counsel, faithful correction and appropriate punishment. This process continued up to the day they left home.

Micah defined the above goal number 2 as:

> He has shown you, O man, what is good;
> And what does the LORD require of you
> But to do justly, to love mercy,
> And to walk humbly with your God?
> *Micah 6:8 NKJV*

Many parents continue to have these two goals after their kids leave. The first tensions between adult children and their parents may come from good parents trying to continue the same job of protecting and guiding.

As good parents intent upon molding good behavior lose their child-parent positional authority, parents are tempted to use other methods of influence. As they feel they are losing control they continue the task of helping their children make the right decisions, using the wrong methods. Almost every parent has unknowingly continued the Adult / Child influence by unwelcomed Pronouncements of dire consequences, if their child continues.

Some parents start to use unrighteous influence. They try to maintain control by; manipulation, guilt trips or self-pity parties. Parents can be quite creative as they continue the process of making good kids.

But the wrong tactics never work correctly. Even when they seem to be working, and stopping their adult children from going down wrong paths, the ultimate goal is missed. The ultimate goal is to have adult children that make the right decisions on their own. You will not always be there to motivate.

As you step back from your goals of parenting your minor children, you will find a new job of parenting. Your newly independent children still need help, and not just to pay their electric bill. Their world still measures out discipline and punishment for wrong behavior.

Defining Your New Job Description
Grandma says, "Say thank you"

When I was 8 years old, my Grandmother lived 5 blocks from our house. I would ride my bicycle to her house most days and she would talk with me. She would give me cookies and nickels to buy candy bars. I learned how to say, "Thank you," from my Grandma.

It was the only thing that she requested. At home the instructions and rules were quite long and I seemed to get in trouble regularly. But at my Grandma's house, she just wanted me to say, "Thank you."

My Grandma died when I was a boy. It was one of the few times I saw my father cry. But I will always remember her delight and smile, when I said, "Thank you Grandma."

Your adult children and their children need you in a new role. They need you to have a new job; a change of your job description. It requires effort and education. In the same way that you looked for help when you first started parenting, you now can learn this new role.

So my wife and I decided to stop one job and look for a new one.

Our job of molding good moral adults was over.
When it looks like we have failed, we ask for forgiveness.
When our children fail in moral areas, we suffer with them.
Our job is over and a new one is just beginning.

We began by defining our new goals as:

1. Regular focused prayer for our grown children and grandchildren.
2. Responsible treatment and wise distribution of our children's physical inheritance.
3. Discerning watchfulness of our children's moral lives.
4. Being an encouragement and support of their directions in life whenever possible.

Understand Who You Have Been
To See Who You Can Be

How blessed is the man who finds wisdom
And the man who gains understanding.
For her profit is better than the profit of silver
And her gain better than fine gold.
Proverbs 3:13-14 NASB

I was struggling with a very strained relationship with one of my adult children. As I drove to a conference, in Los Angeles I started to think, "Your relationship with the church, your wife and family has developed over years into well-defined roles in which you have become comfortable. Over three decades, you have become someone that functions in specific roles and these roles now define how you are relating to your adult children. You try to relate as;

A strong leader
A discerning counselor
An insightful teacher

I continued with the inner voice talking, "This is who you are in all your relationships. When not in one of these roles you feel uncomfortable. When your adult children do not accept you in one of these roles, you go away with a sense of being ineffective.

Your helplessness when not operating in these roles makes you feel you are not being a good father. As a father, you tried to be these three things. You feel powerless if you are not accepted as An effective leader, a wise counselor or a faithful teacher. If you do three things, you can help overcome the impasses you have with your adult children...."

The Problem - You Were a Good Parent

Most successful parents of minor children have well defined roles by the time their children are in their teens. These roles vary greatly by their personalities and life skills. These roles are tweaked some as their children enter teens but they remain largely the same.

Your new role may seem hard to define at first, since most of the things you have been doing have been right. How can you just stop relating in this comfortable parenting role?

My initial prayer on that drive to the LA Conference was, "Why does everything that I do seem to make things worse?" The three things that my inner voice spoke was;

1. Change your role - define a proper role.
2. Focus on speaking blessings from a distance.
3. Continue to move in my old roles with others.

My feeling that everything that I was doing was making things worse had brought me to passivity. Then I would flip to trying harder in my well defined roles. I was making things worse because I was flipping from trying to be in control to being passive and distant.

Giving Them Space and Freedom

Since I had successfully related to most adults in these three positions of authority, I had missed the obvious. My role as the father of my small children had a similar description. My children had for the most part accepted me in those roles as their father as they grew up. Even in their teen years, they had allowed me to be the one who had the right to confront. I would confront in correction and instruction as a father. Since my personality enjoyed being in control, my role as father was structured to remain in this place of control. This dynamic works great for keeping your minor children from running into the street or setting limits to your teenage daughters dating practices.

But all adults have the freedom to accept or reject correction. To accept a parent in the role of corrector or instructor makes young adults feel conflicted about who is in control of their lives. Without realizing it, the roles I had grown to be so comfortable in were perceived as being bad behavior. The rest of the people around me perceived them as helpful and loving.

Let Others Bring Correction

There are four main institutions in our present culture that administers adult instruction, correction and control. These are the government, the church, marriage relationships, and workplace relationships.

In the past there were also three other relationships that exerted pressure upon young adult's behavior. Friends, church community and extended family members use to express approval and disapproval upon newly disconnected adult's life choices. Sadly these three have had their influence eroded largely by my generation.

Parents are not supposed to maintain their confrontational corrective control with their adult children. A part of growing up is having autonomy over one's life. Your children are left with these four institutions to bring discipline where it is needed.

We warn, instruct and correct, with all good intentions, so the unloving governmental authorities of this world do not administer their corrective justice. When they lose their job due to poor behavior, we try to teach them, but the workplace has become their corrector.

It sounds simple. Just redefine your role to a non-corrective, non-confrontational, non-instructive role. Allow your children full control of their lives. But since we have defined our good, helpful behavior as the right behavior, it is hard to stop. Our successes are now our problem areas.

Pray From a Distance and Speak Blessings

No matter what your role, one role that helps mitigate the feeling of helplessness and stops passivity in its tracks is becoming powerful in unseen spiritual realms.

Pray for your children.
Pray through an issue, until you see the resolution.
Pray in the middle of the night when deep concerns awaken you.

Speaking positive blessings over each of your children, helps you stay in the arena of faith and not negative unbelief. It is easy to become negative when you watch your adult children seem to be flailing around making one bad decision after another. When you see the institutions of the world lining up to administer their justice, you experience the pain of your children's failures with them.

As you remain involved in prayer and blessings, it helps you redefine your role. You are no longer just the rescuer. You ask heaven to get involved and then stand back with faith. Faith that God is big enough to help your children, in the same way He helped you. Remember when you were flailing around making poor decisions.

The Second Season

A good man leaves an inheritance
to his children's children *Proverbs 13:22a NASB*

With our present life-spans, the last season of our life may last for decades. All my children were out of the house when I was 53 years old. Assuming that I am an average North American, I will live into my 80's. This second season will last over 30 years. This is longer than the 29 years from the birth of my first child to my last child leaving home. You have time to make new habits and learn new ways of relating.

Your Job Is Done

Making New Habits

It is a myth that it only takes 21 days of repetition to make a new habit. There has been much study on human willpower and the ability to break bad habits and make good ones. Replace your old behavior with new habits.

The book Willpower by Roy F. Baumeister and John Tierney has many solid principles to help you achieve new habits in your new roles. They found that two things dramatically help form new habits. These are monitoring and accountability. Find someone to help you monitor your desired changes and then give them permission to speak into your life in these areas. Be honest and accountable to your monitor.

Here is a list that my wife and I developed to help monitor each other's behavior.

1. We will guard against negative talk of any kind. We will bless our children each day, with renewed faith that God will take our blessings and help our children endure the consequences of their decisions, good and bad. When bad things happen, we will speak about the problem with faith.

2. We will avoid our normal parental roles of correction and instruction. We will not offer advice, unless asked. We will watch to see when our children are comfortable with our opinion being expressed.

3. We will carefully consider when and if we should rescue our children. We will view our rescuing them from their actions as a behavior that may cause more harm than good. We will respect the authority the four institutions mentioned above.

4. We will be verbally supportive and encouraging, whenever possible. We will recognize our own feelings of guilty when our children fail. We will remind each other that failure can bring wisdom and success to our children.

5. Finally, we will look for new ways to relate to outside our comfort zones, but within our own personalities. We will watch for confusion or our reverting back to old behaviors.

Continue to Help Others
Function in Your God Given Gifts

God has blessed you with skills and gifts to help others. Continue to seek out other relationships to fill the vacuum that was created as you gave your children space. God is not asking you to change your role in the church or even in the rest of your family.

Ask God to help you see the new things that He has for you to do in this new season. Your days of active parenting minors, took up large amounts of your resources and time. In this new season you do not have to plan your life around the day to day activities of your children. You have extra time. Use it to grow, learn and bless others.

So what about this new role?

The next chapter explores what it means to function in a different kind of authority; the Biblical Patriarch.

3

Your New Authority
The Biblical Patriarch

There was a man in the land of Uz whose name was Job;
and that man was blameless, upright,
fearing God and turning away from evil.
JOB 1:1 NASB

There was a man in the land of Uz who God bragged about to everyone in Heaven. This is an amazing story, since this man, named Job was also one of the richest men on the Earth. He had walked with God, for many years of testing and serving God to achieve the place of God bragging about him to the Heavenly hosts.

There is not much said about Job's life before the short time of testing that is the main subject his book. One of the few things that we are told is that Job prayed for and offered sacrifices for his adult children regularly. These prayers had been answered by God by God putting a hedge of protection around his adult children.

His vigilance in watching over his seven adult sons' and three adult daughters' spiritual states is one of the things mentioned about Job's specific behavior. This was a part of Job's behavior that God loved. He was faithful to not assume that his children were doing OK in their relationship with God. It could be implied that Job's adult children were the same as all of our children; independent but still needing Job.

Parental authority is a special authority. Your position as parent is recognized by God through all of life's seasons. Your relationship is so important to God that He included it as a protected relationship in one of His 10 moral laws. It is the first Commandment that has a specific promise to all those who obey it.

A quick review of the different kinds of authority is helpful as we define your authority as a parent of adult children. I am calling this authority the authority of a patriarch. Because the practice of a parents authority changes as their children disconnect, it is helpful to understand authority different types of spiritual and positional authority.

A Quick Study of Authority
Human Authority

I Peter 2:12-14 describes several agencies of human authority. Whenever appropriate we are to submit to these authorities. There are government authorities such as police and bureaucracies, or other less powerful agencies of authority such as school teachers, business managers, and homeowners associations.

The facility managers of most churches would be considered having human authority (not spiritual authority) over the physical buildings they are responsible to manage. Human authority is positional and associated with what the person is responsible for. It is dependent upon the badge being worn at the time.

The assistant manager at Walmart has authority to tell you to not travel down an aisle while it is wet. If he quits his job, he has no authority to tell you anything. His authority reaches to the Walmart property line. When you leave the Walmart parking lot, he has no authority over you.

I attend some churches that prohibit coffee being brought into the sanctuary of the church. I also attend churches that allow coffee to be brought into the sanctuary. This arbitrary rule is enforced with human authority.

The nature of human authority is that it should be limited to the position and the responsibility areas of the authority. If human authority over reaches, rebellion grows until the position is taken away.

Spiritual Authority with Men

The authority that God gives Pastors and other Christian Ministers is an authority that gives specific men the ability to influence other men. This position of influence is always voluntary. Each man is free to relate to Godly leaders and listen to what they have to say.

Mature Christians submit to spiritual authority with thoughtful discernment. The pastors and church ministries that have this authority should exercise it without manipulation, seduction, or a controlling attitude.

> If to others I *(Paul)* am not an apostle,
> at least I am to you... *I Corinthians 9:2 NASB*

> *(Peter to the Elders of the church)*
> Shepherd the flock of God among you,
> exercising oversight not under compulsion,
> but voluntarily... *I Peter 5:2 NASB*

These two scriptures illustrate the freedom all Christians have in choosing the men that they accept as Spiritual Authorities. Not everyone in the 1st Century Church related to Paul as an apostle. Even though he wrote a large portion of the New Testament, the Apostle Paul had authority only when it was recognized. Peter as a fellow elder flatly states that those who serve in positions of authority should do so voluntarily.

Spiritual Authority in Unseen Realms

All believers have spiritual authority over the realms of darkness when they represent the Kingdom of God. The Bible teaches that some human events are influenced in our visible world by prayers. It is this authority that Job walked in as he offered sacrifices to God for the sake of his children. God had "Hedged" them with protection and satan was powerless because of Job's prayers.

Parental Authority

Parental authority starts as "Human Authority." As parents we have responsibility to protect, instruct, punish and discipline our children within Biblical guidelines. Our love for our kids compels us to continue in this human care, even after they leave home. As our children become independent adults, we lose our human authority. Human authority is defined by responsibility. When you are no longer responsible for your children, you no longer have human authority.

> Children, obey your parents as the Lord wants, because this is the right thing to do. The command says, "Honor your father and mother." This is the first command that has a promise with it— "Then everything will be well with you, and you will have a long life on the earth." *Ephesians 6:1-3 NCV*

Ephesians 6:1 talks about the response required toward human authority – obedience. Verse 2 then continues quoting the 5th Commandment. This command to honor can only be fully obeyed as a child grows old enough to understand the concept of conditional honor, respect and trust. My book *The Hidden Promise, Honoring Your Parents* explores in detail the distinction between obeying and honoring.

It is here where Parental authority is given a special place in all other relationships. This Patriarchal Authority is distinct and different from all other types of authority. When your child becomes an independent adult, you continue in a God given positional authority. It is similar to the defined Spiritual Authority above.

The guidelines of this new authority are stated in I Peter 5:2. There is an "exercising" of this authority as a shepherd would over his flock of sheep. This authority should be embraced voluntarily, not with an attitude that you are being forced to serve.

Your New Authority

When a parent's authority changes from "Human Authority" to "Positional Spiritual Authority" a parent must exert effort and exercise this new authority. It is not automatic. As you had to exercise authority over your minor children, telling them to not run into the street, you must also exercise this new authority.

The exercising of spiritual authority is different. As a parent of a dependent child, you had every right to enforce your edicts with, "Because I am your father." It is good to have other reasons for rules. But there are times when a parent stops reasoning and exercises their authority. They are responsible, for the welfare and actions of their child. They have the final say. The exercising of positional spiritual authority has different dynamics.

Patriarchal Authority is successful when practiced in a similar way that Positional Spiritual Authority is practiced.

1. Actions should be motivated by the love for those being served.
2. Actions should be free from selfish motives.
3. Actions should be free from hidden motives.
4. An availability and openness to serve.
5. A sacrificial faithfulness to serve.

Our unselfish love brings us to the throne of God, as our children's intercessors. As Job asked for God's protection in his children's lives, so we also stand before God asking for His power.

> Your kingdom come, your will be done
> On earth as it is in heaven.
> *Matthew 6:10 NASB*

As we stand in a place of intercession for our children, we begin by asking for God's will to be done in their lives. We ask that God's Kingdom will be established in our children's lives in the same way that it is established in Heaven.

> Now this is the confidence we have before Him: Whenever we ask anything according to His will, He hears us. And if we know that He hears whatever we ask, we know that we have what we have asked Him for. *I John 5:14-15 HCSB*

As we pray for God's will for our children, we are directed by the Holy Spirit to not just pray for protection, but also that they would succeed in walking the path that God has for them – God's will on this Earth.

Faith Filled Authority
Developing Eyes of Faith

> Now when the attendant of the man of God had risen early and gone out, behold, an army with horses and chariots was circling the city. And his servant said to him, "Alas, my master! What shall we do?" So he answered, "Do not fear, for those who are with us are more than those who are with them."

> Then Elisha prayed and said, "O LORD, I pray, open his eyes that he may see." And the LORD opened the servant's eyes and he saw; and behold, the mountain was full of horses and chariots of fire all around Elisha. *II Kings 6:15-17 NASB*

As parents it is easy to see the problems. We are so close to the problem that we can see the enemy's "army." Most parents need to develop eyes of faith. Eyes that see God's power and plan as more powerful than all the negatives we see in the natural realms. As we begin to pray for specific problems, God hears our prayers and begins to respond to accomplish His will in our children's lives. Our prayers begin unseen and God directed events.

If we only look to see visible immediate results, we can become disheartened or confused, while God's processes work. As two chemicals that mix and produce unseen results, so our prayers mix with God's unseen power to produce a change in temporal events in our children's lives. But those changes may not be seen immediately.

It is wonderful when we see immediate results to our prayers. But God's Spirit moves upon our children in the same way He moves upon all adults. He never bullies us into conforming to His wise rules. God's unseen actions respect our children's free will.

Growing In Your New Authority
The Process

The process of growing in your parental authority started many years ago. If you are like me, you told your 2 year old not to _____. Then you learned to react with loving correction when ignored. You told your 5 year old to not run into the street. You educated yourself and learned how to discipline correctly. We discovered that each of our children is different and began to relate in different ways to each of them.

This process of growing into more authority as your children grew into more complicated circumstances seemed to be automatic at times. Out of necessity, you grew into more understanding of how to administer parental authority. As more children came into the family, the job seemed to get easier. Then it seemed everything you had learned no longer worked with your pre-teen or teens.

With preteens we learned that punishment was more effective when it involved taking away something that they wanted. We learned to not take everything away at the same time or we would have no leverage. We learned the more complicated rules of disciplining teens.

With our teens we learned to talk with another person that just needed to disagree with us. We learned to accept their opinions when they were arbitrary and unfounded. We tried to learn and sometimes succeeded in maintaining control as our leverage diminished.

Now it is time to discover more. This time the process of growing in influence and authority continues, but there are no cookie-cutter answers. This time to exercise authority you will need not just knowledge but also wisdom. This book is written to help you in the process.

Carrying the Weight of Authority

The church meeting was somber. Everyone who regularly attended was there, except for the younger Christians who had already joined other churches. It was the last service of a group of people who had met together for decades. Some had been there for 30 years.

I had been the main pastor of this group for 25 years. I had had a great time, meeting with Christians who loved God and loved to worship. I had had a great time bringing a fresh message each week to meet their hearts and strengthen them in their Kingdom endeavors. And now there was an end to the season. This was my last service with this group.

As the church service ended, I walked into the Pastors Study immediately off the sanctuary. A strange sensation came over me. I was unprepared for it. I felt a weight lift off my shoulders; an almost physical sensation of being lighter.

Immediately a thought came to my mind. My 5th child had just left home. The responsibility of leading the church had been like having a 5th child. Because I had carried the authority of being pastor for so long, the weight had become a natural thing to carry. Now the weight was gone.

When your kids left and started making a life separate from you, you might have also felt a weight lift. Or if the process was slow, with stutter steps (they moved out and then back in) you may have only felt relief as they finally got out on their own.

But whatever your experience, you need to pick up and carry a new weight of authority; the weight of carrying the authority of the Patriarch of your family. It may take you a few years to understand how to function in this authority. But the job is yours if you wish to take it.

It is my prayer that you will be a wise and loving patriarch of your children, grandchildren and great-grandchildren. God has given you a promise. If you ask, He will give you wisdom. It is my prayer that you will grow in the wisdom of God in this new season.

> But if any of you lacks wisdom,
> Let him ask of God,
> Who gives to all generously
> And without reproach,
> And it will be given to him.
> *James 1:5 NASB*

4

Rising Above the Temporal
Acting with God's Love

For by these He has granted to us His precious and
magnificent promises, so that by them you may
become **partakers of the divine nature**, having escaped
the corruption that is in the world by lust. *II Peter 1:4 NASB*

I have a difficult time loving everyone. There are people who are lovable and there are people who are not loveable. Some people just get on my nerves and I have to pray for grace to tolerate them, especially if they are in the church I attend.

And then there are people whom I avoid. This is what makes the story of Jesus so amazing. He did not avoid people. His heart was full of love toward "The Rich Young Ruler" in Matthew 19. When the young man turned down Jesus' personal invitation to become one of his disciples, Jesus still loved him.

Jesus did not avoid the lepers, the beggars, the hated tax collectors or the leaders of His religion who hated him. This ability to have supernatural love for the unlovable is a part of the Divine Nature promised to us in the above passage. This same ability has been promised to you. Although we may all fall far short of this exhibition of the divine nature we should still set it as our goal. Our goal as Christian parents is to be Christ-like toward our children; to act as Christ would act.

Don't Be a Curmudgeon

Rejoice with those who rejoice,
And weep with those who weep.
Romans 12:15 NASB

Rising Above The Temporal

As a person grows older and has more and more experiences they either become wiser or are changed in negative ways. There is a danger that we all may change into "Joy Stealers." A Joy Stealer is a person who has a hard time rejoicing with those who rejoice.

Do you exhibit curmudgeon behavior? Your adult daughter is excited about a new television program. It is a Cop / buddy / action comedy. She would like you to enjoy it as much as she is enjoying it. Her excitement is real. But you have already been watching cop / secret agent / buddy / action / comedy TV shows for 50 years.

You are not impressed by these new actors doing the same thing, sometimes using the same lines. Your negative reaction steals your daughter's excitement. You are acting like a curmudgeon.

The fact that you have been paying attention and have an average intellect can propel you faster into the world of the Joy Stealers. The scriptures are quite clear when addressing how we are to treat those who are older. But now almost everyone you interact with is younger.

Now That Everyone Is Younger

The answer to the problem of everyone being younger than you is to learn to be more gracious. Learn to rejoice with those who rejoice. Unless something is dangerous or illegal, it is not important that you are not impressed. Be gracious when interacting with your adult children.

Don't be the curmudgeon who becomes hardened to life's pains. Mourn with those who mourn. Your son calls and is deeply distressed over something that seems like such a small thing to you. Try to not minimize his distress. The flip side of being a Joy Stealer is being a Minimizer.

If you live long enough, you will probably have more bad things happen to you than everyone around you. You have already overcome many of life's difficulties. You have learned to not stress the small stuff. And most stuff you regard as small. Your kids haven't learned that. They will. But until they do, mourn with those who mourn.

People don't like sharing their problems with a minimizer. As a young man I cringed each time I heard an older person say, "Been there, done that." No matter what the problem was, it seemed that some older people lacked an ability to empathize with my predicament. The fact that they had been through worse, did not help me with my present problem. The curmudgeon does not feel that he has any responsibility to mourn with those who mourn.

Don't minimize other's troubles. No matter what your initial reaction, be the one who can give a balanced response when asked. Be the one who can be counted upon to be a strength in the time of the storm. Be the one who encourages by building courage to weather life's trials.

I fell asleep at a movie with my grandson. He thought it was the best 3 hours he had ever experienced. To him it was the most awesome movie he had ever seen. When I was asked my opinion, the only thing I remember saying was, "It was too long." My lack of joy did not hurt our relationship but now, thinking back, I wish I had been more gracious. It would not have been hard for me to enjoy what he was enjoying, just because he was enjoying it. I wish I hadn't reacted like an old curmudgeon.

God's Love Manifested in Patience

But the fruit of the Spirit is love,
Joy, peace, patience, *Galatians 5:22a*

Have Patience with your adult children. This is one of the fruits of the Holy Spirit. Choose to act patiently. Ask God to give you the ability to be patient, as you choose to be patient. Exhibiting Divine Nature abilities are not automatic to the Christian. You must reach for, accept and walk in the promise.

Most people learn things by trial and error. Our desire as parents would be to see our kids learn from our wise counsel and always decide correctly. But your kids are probably like mine, normal. There will be times that they have wrong thinking; make wrong choices; choose wrong actions as they learn and get their priorities correct.

We all want our children to live with good judgment. But the process of developing good judgment is sometimes two steps forward and one step back. Growing in wisdom does not have to be as hard as some of our kids make it. And that is why we ask for patience.

Some of the mistakes of judgment that you observe will be easy to ignore.
Learning when to not neglect the automobile oil change;
Keeping the backseat clear of fast food wrappers;
Staying up too late and missing work needlessly;

But other mistakes will require "Divine Nature Patience." Galatians 5:22a in the New King James Version uses the word longsuffering instead of patience. It is an appropriate translation. Longsuffering means suffering for an extended period of time. You may need the heart quality of longsuffering. In my personal experience, all suffering seems long. My heart goes out to parents who suffer for extended periods of time with their children.

God's Love Manifested in Self-control

The fruit of the Spirit is ... self-control
Galatians 5:22-23 HSCB

Like apples of gold in settings of silver
is a word spoken in right circumstances.
Proverbs 25:11 NASB

As the parent of a minor child you have learned there are times that you should not help. This takes self-control. In most instances with your younger children, maintaining an appropriate response may only require a small amount of self-control.

We temper our actions and reactions to all adults in our world. We manifest self-control each day as things happen around us. Treat your child as you would treat other adults. Learn self-control and respect your child's right to be an adult.

Can you stop yourself from the life-long habit of pointing out what is obvious to you? God will help you have self-control to stop- STOP- **STOP** and think before you speak; before you offer your advice. Most adults do not like unsolicited advice.

Be ready to pour out the years of experience that can help your children avoid the mistakes and pitfalls you have made, WHEN THEY ASK. Wait for the right circumstances to speak and it will be accepted as something very valuable, "Like apples of gold in settings of silver."

If your relationship is strained and you don't know why;
If your daughter says to you, "Mom, I'm not a child anymore;"
If your child says, "You're always butting in;"
It is time to stop and use self-control.

Your goal is to have the best relationship that you can have with your adult child. There may come a time in the future when your child will accept your wisdom as something valuable. They may mature and perceive your unsolicited advice as something that you do out of your great love for them. But until that happens learn self-control.

Finally a wise man knows when to listen. Encourage your adult children to share their feelings; share their opinions about scripture; share their understanding about life and listen, without commenting. By just listening you may gain a new understanding of your child's thinking.

God's Love Manifested
In Kindness and Gentleness

The fruit of the Spirit is… kindness … gentleness…
Galatians 5:22-23 NASB (selected)

The fruit of the Holy Spirit of kindness and gentleness is exhibited in the underlying tone of your relationship and the small acts directed toward your children.

Look for times that you can intentionally perform acts of kindness. Write a nice note in birthday cards or Christmas cards. Write about your love and appreciation. Speak positive words of how proud you are of an accomplishment. Look for things that they need and give it to them before they ask. Each of your children is impacted differently by acts of kindness. If possible learn what impacts their heart. Is it small gifts? Is it cards and notes? Find ways to be kind.

When you confront things that you feel must be spoken, be gentle in your tone and your words. Your goal is to have a good relationship with another adult, not win the argument. You can gently and respectfully disagree.

If you have been a strong disciplinarian, your adult child may have only "child" memories of you. Their childhood memories are probably not fully correct. They may view you as someone who acts harshly only because of childhood perceptions.

Your gentleness and kindness can bring a balanced perspective to your young adult's heart. It may show the truth that your discipline was only for their good. You can defuse the tension of the situation with acts of kindness; kindness with no hidden motives. Just do something nice.

God's Love Manifested in Humility

With all humility and gentleness, with patience,
Showing tolerance for one another in love,
Being diligent to preserve the
Unity of the Spirit in the bond of peace.
Ephesians 4:2-3 NASB

Learn to embrace humility. As a parent of smaller children, it was important that you were right most of the time. Even when you were wrong, they didn't know it. If you found, you had made an error, you could repent and immediately take the position of being right again. But with adults, you do not have to be right all the time.

One of my spiritual mentors defined humility as, "Not insisting upon your own rightness." A humble person is not concerned with how they are perceived at any given moment.

In most families parents are given the above assignment – "*to preserve the unity of the Spirit in the bond of peace.*" Families can begin to have disunity long before relationships break. You can be right with the wrong attitude. It is better to be right with humility, gentleness and patience. Embrace humility. When your opinion is rejected, God will give you the grace of humility – "*showing tolerance for one another in love.*"

Asking for and Accepting God's Forgiveness

Train up a child in the way he should go,
And when he is old he will not depart from it.
Proverbs 22:6 NKJV

There are no perfect parents. And the fact that you were not perfect may bring your child to the culturally incorrect conclusion. "I am the way I am, because my parents screwed me up." This stupid idea is opposite to Christian doctrine. Bad parents have great kids and good parents have horrible kids.

But some of your mistakes have affected your children. Questioning parental mistakes and shortcomings is a part of the process of growing up. When done correctly, this process helps children avoid repeating some of the mistakes their parents have made. This process of questioning started in adolescents and it continues into your child's twenties and thirties.

With all your love and with all your sacrifices, you made mistakes and now your adult child may want to talk about those mistakes. I recommend the following approach to this potential mine field of discovery.

1. Admit what you see as valid mistakes.
2. Ask those involved for forgiveness without minimizing the mistake.
3. Ask for God's forgiveness.
4. Forgive yourself.
5. Then accept God's forgiveness.

A quality of humility is not placing your feelings or actions above God's ability to handle them. God is a God of new beginnings. Take this normal process of your adult children questionings and make this one of God's new beginnings in your life.

If you think it will help, write a letter about some of the mistakes that your children have voiced. If your child is stuck on something you did or didn't do, address the item, humbly. You may be able to help them work through forgiving and having a new beginning too.

What to Hide From Your Children

You know what the really big failures were. Hopefully your children were sheltered from these mistakes. There is no reason to discuss things that your children are unaware of. Take your big failures to God, to a friend or to your counselor.

Most children are not objective enough to be their parent's counselor. It might make you feel good to get everything out in the open, but if it doesn't help them, keep it to yourself. Much, much later in life, you might have an opportunity to help your 40 or 50 year old children understand your reaction to the failures of others; or ask for forgiveness for your own failures.

Read Proverbs 22:6 with the right emphasis. "Train up a child in the way he should go and **WHEN HE IS OLD** he will not depart from it." This Proverb's promise is that youthful instruction will make a difference in children's lives once they have reached maturity – when they are old. We all pray that maturity comes quickly and the time when they stumble quickly passes. But don't allow guilt and condemnation to torment you because your kids are struggling. Accept God's forgiveness and get on with life.

God's Love Manifested in Forgiveness

Then Peter came and said to Him, "Lord, how often shall my brother sin against me and I forgive him? Up to seven times?" Jesus said to him, "I do not say to you, up to seven times, but up to seventy times seven.
Matthew 18:21-22 NASB

Identify the unforgiven offenses within your heart, by recognizing the area that still hurts. You might be able to understand the reason certain things happened, but forgiveness does not require an explanation. Ask God to help you let go of the pain and negative feelings, whether your child repents or not. Then you will be ready with a heart of love, when they do repent.

Repentance of past offenses is a part of having a good relationship. You should not minimize the importance of your adult child's asking for forgiveness for past sins against you. But you do not have to wait for them to ask.

They remain guilty before God until they repent. You should pray for their attitude to change. You should pray that they ask you and others for forgiveness. But you can be released from the prison of your own resentment, no matter what attitude your children have.

You can stop holding the sin against them. This is the definition of Christian forgiveness. Carrying a grudge for years can hurt you more than the party that has offended you.

5
Inspiring Your Kid's Kids
Adam's Inspiration to Enoch

Adam lived one hundred and thirty years, and begot a son in
his own likeness, after his image, and named him Seth....
Enoch lived sixty-five years, and begot Methuselah.

After he begot Methuselah, Enoch walked with God three
hundred years, and had sons and daughters. So all the days of
Enoch were three hundred and sixty-five years. And Enoch
walked with God; and he was not, for God took him.
Genesis 5:3, 21-24 NASB

Adam was the great, great, great, great grandfather of Enoch.
Adam died 3 years after Enoch was translated into heaven
without dying. Enoch's son, Methuselah lived to be the oldest
man that has ever lived on the Earth and was the grandfather of Noah.
There were three men, before the flood that the scripture calls out as
walking with God. They were Adam, Enoch and Noah.

Noah was a righteous man, blameless among his
contemporaries; Noah walked with God.
Genesis 6:9b HCSB

Enoch grew up with a large extended family. He had four grandfathers
with the senior grandfather being Adam. I assume that Adam would
regularly sit in the evening and talk about the days of living in the
Garden of Eden. The days that he walked with God in paradise and
what it was like to live in a world with no sin, no disease and no
futility. Adam's influence upon the immediate generations after him,
are shown in God's description of them.

By faith Enoch was taken away so that he did not see
death, "and was not found, because God had taken him"; for
before he was taken he had this testimony, that he pleased God.

But without faith it is impossible to please Him, for he who
comes to God must believe that He is, and that He is a rewarder
of those who diligently seek Him. *Hebrews 11:5-6 NKJV*

It was probably the stories of walking with God in the garden that made a great impact upon Enoch as a young adult and father. Adam imparted to his son and grandsons the heart to avoid the sin of the age and walk with God each day. His story of the wonderful fellowship with God and the regret of losing that fellowship must have motivated his grandson, Enoch to seek that same closeness.

Enoch walked with this diligent seeking of God and gained a testimony that he pleased God and became the first man to live "life into life," and not die. For 300 years he would talk with Adam about relating to God outside the dark world that had been subjected to futility.

Adam died three years after Enoch was taken to heaven. Noah was the first of the generations that would not see or hear the firsthand accounts of the Garden of Eden from Adam. But the generational impact of having the patriarchs in the family walk with God continued.

A good man leaves an inheritance to his grandchildren,
but the sinner's wealth is stored up for the righteous.
Proverbs 13:22 NCSB

Grandparents and great grandparents are important to future generation's spiritual growth. This inheritance is in three arenas of life; physical, emotional and spiritual.

Your relationship to your adult children directly affects your impact on your grandchildren and great grandchildren. If your relationship is strained due to moral failures or personality problems, it is not your prerogative to walk away – not if there are grandchildren.

Respect the Young Family's Rules

Do nothing from selfishness or empty conceit, but with humility of mind **regard one another as more important than yourselves**; do not merely look out for your own personal interests, but also for the interests of others.
Philippians 2:3-4 NASB

Let love be without hypocrisy. Abhor what is evil; cling to what is good. Be devoted to one another in brotherly love; **give preference to one another in honor**; not lagging behind in diligence, fervent in spirit, serving the Lord;
Romans 12:9-11 NASB

To have a blessed relationship with your child's family, it is important to respect their family rules. The temptation to disrespect their preferences as silly puts strain on the relationship. When you respect your adult child's authority over their home, it is easier for your adult child to give you more honor. Your authority as a grandparent is determined partially by how much honor you are given by your adult children.

Clarify your child's "family rules," and then follow them with the right attitude. As you learned how to parent minors by being in agreement to your spouse, be in agreement with your child's authority to set limits and establish order in their house.

New parents are learning the same way you learned - by doing. They are learning how to carry authority and enforce rules. What to eat, when to go to bed, what to watch on TV, may be much more important to the new parents than these rules are to you. Your child may be a little too uptight or over protective with their first or second child. But consider them as more important than yourself. They will mellow, just like you probably mellowed.

Instead of pointing out the obvious, that they are going way overboard at providing new monitoring devices or keeping their baby on a strict schedule, allow them to develop by respecting their opinion over yours. They have brothers, sisters, and friends that will point out the obvious to them. Except in extreme cases, just relax and let your child learn as you learned.

Following Them around the Country

Dennis Prager asked parents of adult children to call into his national radio show and answer this question, "How close to your adult children should you live?" One caller described how he had quit his job in Chicago and moved with his wife to Phoenix to be closer to the grandchildren. After a few years, his child was now moving their family one thousand miles away. What could he do?

There may be a reason why your children live far from you. There is no ideal distance that you should live from your grandchildren. Geographic closeness does not bring emotional closeness. In my family alone, three generations have had siblings live next door to each other. In every case the emotionally broken, yet controlling adult in the family encouraged their siblings that it would be great to live next door. In every case, they ended up moving, as they realized that geographic closeness does not bring emotional closeness. A little distance can do wonders for family harmony.

The Active Adult Syndrome

Motor homes all over America display the bumper sticker, "I'm spending my children's inheritance." Meant to be humorous, it shows the Baby Boomer's self-centered attitudes toward the next generation. Our present culture teaches grandparents to accomplish their bucket list. I am not against doing special things, traveling and seeing the world. But grandparents should be doing much more for the world than checking off things from their bucket list.

Retiring earlier with decades of good health, grandparents have been encouraged to stay active. But in their activity, their grandchildren may see them less. When the last child left our home, my wife and I went through the normal, predicable transition. Our lives had revolved around our children's schedules. Now we had our own schedules. It was weird to realize that we could go here or there and no one cared. It had been a long time since we had done something with first telling someone what we planned; how long it would take; when we would be back. Our new freedom felt weird.

This second life of freedom is great when your health is good and you have the money that gives you many options. Combine a busy career that will continue for the next decade and your availability to share your grandchildren's lives can be greatly limited. Set being a grandparent as one of the stewardships of your new life. Make it a priority. If you live a distance away, take vacations near the grandkids. Find times to interact on Face Book or Skype.

From the correct distance, maintain a loving and respectful relationship with your adult child for your grandkids sake. Then become the one with another point of view, just when they need another point of view. When your grandkids are in elementary school, it is wonderful to be there for them. But when they are struggling through the teenage years, your advice could be the difference between shipwreck or success.

The Malachi Curse in This Generation

"Behold, I am going to send you Elijah the prophet before the
coming of the great and terrible day of the Lord. He
will restore the hearts of the fathers to their children and the
hearts of the children to their fathers, so that I will not come
and smite the land with a curse." *Malachi 4:5-6 NASB*

The last two verses of the Old Testament point to the last generations that will live on Earth before Jesus' triumphal return. The curse that comes when each generation rejects the generation before them is one of the natural outcomes of not having grandparents. Their wise input about past mistakes can bring valuable insight to future generations.

Recently the words of Malachi have proven true in our culture. Adult children are fully disconnecting from their parents. The brokenness of families is one of the signs of the times we live in. Baring criminal behavior, if your child will not let you see your grandchildren, they are deeply broken emotionally at best and at worst an immoral person.

Stopping all contact between grandparents and grandchildren is an immoral act, since it breaks one of the Ten Commandments. The moral impact of denying future generations a good relationship with past generations may be worse than breaking some of the more obvious commandments. It is our country's shame that we have cowardly Christian leadership who do not confront this devastating practice throughout their congregations.

The World's Going to Hell in a Hand Basket
God's Promise That Breaks Generational Deterioration

"You shall not make for yourself an idol… You shall not
worship them or serve them; for I, the LORD your God, am
a jealous God, visiting the iniquity of the fathers on the
children, on the third and the fourth generations of those who
hate Me, but showing lovingkindness to thousands, to those
who love Me and keep My commandments.
Exodus 20:4-6 NASB

God has promised to show love to generation after generation after generation to a "thousand generations" to those who keep His commandments. It is easy to see the curse of sin "To the third and fourth generations." We see similar bad behavior continue in a family generation after generation. One family has problems with gambling; another has problems with sexual sins; another is affected by deep emotional problems. DNA alone does not account for the affect that each generation has upon the next.

God has the answer and it is grandparents. We can do what no one else can do. We can be faithful witnesses to our children's children and hopefully to our great grandchildren.

Perfection Is Not Necessary

Your children due to deception, brokenness or just silliness may fall prey to the idea that it is better to have "problem free" people around their family. I describe in Chapter 4 of my book, *The Hidden Promise, Honoring Your Parents*, the blessings of having imperfect people in your family.

Parents have many faults, some bigger than others. It is the failures of those in the family that teach your grandchildren life lessons. They learn to be genuine Christians, as they observe how you and your children react, love, forgive and struggle with the imperfections and failures of relatives. To try to isolate the family for imperfection is futile and wrong.

If we Christians cannot live a life of forgiveness toward our close relatives, including our parents and grandparents, who can? Christians are required to begin their spiritual journey with repentance. Christians start with a declaration of imperfection and their need for forgiveness and fixing.

Parents should influence their children to always pick friends with the realization that friends influence friends. Good people influence others toward goodness. Bad people influence others toward bad behavior. But isolating one generation from the other using this principle negates the higher principle of honoring parents.

Does God not care that there is a possibility that past generations can corrupt the future generations by teaching wrong behavior? The Bible is full of just that scenario. But according to Malachi 4:5-6 one of the worst behaviors that can be taught is the disconnection of the generations through self-centered and cold hearts toward those who are the most close to us.

Malachi talks about a time that will come on the Earth when parents will no longer have love toward their children and where their children will have no heart of love toward their parents. This will be the greatest time of deception that has ever existed upon the Earth. God will take, as explained in Chapter 1 - Principle 1, extraordinary steps to stop this curse from coming upon the Earth.

You and I can be a part of this great promise being fulfilled. We can corporate with God's power and vision for this Earth and be a part of the healing of the generations. When you find a friend struggling with honoring their imperfect parents, be a healing influence. When you find an estranged adult child, encourage them to work out their problems with their parents.

Do not fall prey to the foolishness of one generations justifying sinful behavior toward another. In the companion book to this book, I explain how every generation can honor the past generation.

Have the best relationship with your child that you can have, for the sake of your grandkids.

6

The Pain of Disappointment
Defining Your Expectations

R ichard Lapchick is the son of Joe Lapchick. Joe Lapchick was the original center on the Boston Celtic NBA Basketball team. As a young man, Richard Lapchick had suffered an injury and his father was upset to hear a friend comment about his son, "Richard may never play basketball again." Implying that Richard would not accomplish what his father had accomplished in the NBA.

His father replied that if his son, Joe was never successful at basketball, it would not matter to him. He wanted Richard to be a good person, who made a difference with his life. His son did not have to play professional basketball to make him happy.

This comment freed Richard to become a successful ESPN Commentator and prolific author about sports and social issues. Until he heard this from his dad, he was confused about what his father's expectations were.

Defining the expectations you have for your children is important to them and to you. Communicating your love and support and releasing them to find God's path will bring clarity to them, as it did with Richard Lapchick.

I have had many times of confusion about how to react to my children's life choices. Even though I assumed that this confusion was normal, it did not lessen my emotional distress. Undefined disappointment can be like a low grade fever to a relationship. If the relationship is already distant or strained, the pain of disappointment can overwhelm your positive feelings for your child.

The Pain of Disappointment

Compared to the ups and downs of childhood, adult children's life choices can be much more devastating. The effect of wrong decisions can last for decades. It is because of our love for them that we worry. So we pray. We lose sleep and we become disappointed.

Define Your Expectations

My child, if you are wise, then I will be happy.
I will be so pleased, if you speak what is right.
Proverbs 23:15-16 NCV

There are typical expectations that most parents have. We want our children to be happy, educated, successful, independent, and morally good. We want them to grow up to be mature enough to be responsible for themselves and others. We hope that they will find a good spouse and be happy in their nuclear family.

Then there are specific expectations that vary greatly from one family to another. These expectations may include:

Graduating from college	Having a professional career
Getting married	Having a large family
Being an exceptional parent	Being in a Christian Ministry

The list can go on and on and is as varied as the families who define them. As Richard Lapchick needed to hear his father Joe, say that it was OK to not be an NBA basketball player; your children need to hear you express your expectations.

My Expectation List

Top Expectations
1. Be a person who love's God and has a good relationship with Him.
2. Be a moral person who treats others the way God wants.

Important Expectations
1. Grow emotionally mature and take care of yourself and your dependents.
2. Become responsible with your money, time and energy.
3. Serve and help others, not just themselves and their families.

Wish List of Expectations
1. Grow and become excellent in the areas of their skills.
2. Have a happy marriage and a stable lifestyle.
3. Have children and be a good parent.
4. Have a good relationship with their family, friends and church.

As you make your own Expectations List, start your list with general expectations for all your children. Then, if you are able, make the list specific to each of your children. Have appropriate expectations of your child's growth in the important things.

There are things that are out of your child's ability to control. Make your important or top expectations things that they can choose to do. For example my wish list for my kids is to have children, be a good parent and have a happy family. But these things can be affected by other's failure. We hope for many things for our kids. But the most important things should be defined to them throughout their formative years.

Define your top expectations and don't lower them. Keep the bar high. Expectations should be appropriate for each of your children's ages, personalities and present season of life. As you watch your children grow up, encourage them to succeed in the important things first.

Find an Objective Perspective

We would all look at someone who expected their 2nd grader to do Calculus, as having inappropriate expectations. If your neighbor expected their High School student to play basketball in the NBA, we would shake our heads, unless your neighbor was Joe Bryant (Kobe Bryant's father.) Free yourself from inappropriate expectations and you will free yourself from unrealistic disappointments.

The Pain of Disappointment

If you failed in this process of expressing your expectations, talk with your child. Free them to forge their own path in life, with correct values. If you have inverted the important with the "might be nice" expectations, talk with your child about what you feel is the most important things in life.

If possible, develop a way to express your expectations regularly, while they are still at home. Repeat yourself. Find other resources that lead young people to correct moral thinking. Your parental expectations are being enforced daily to your minor children. But day to day expectations like, "Do your homework," does not translate to future expectations for adults.

Be intentional when telling your young children your future expectations. "When you leave home, I hope you find a great wife," is a future expectation. "The most important thing to me, son, is that you learn to make right judgments." Stop the pain of undefined disappointment, by being intentional.

Negative Comments Attached to Our Pain

"Cobie" Smolders is the Canadian actress that played Robin on the Television Sitcom, *How I Met Your Mother*. On the show, Robin's character has an interesting back story. Her father wanted a son so he named her Robin Charles Scherbatsky Jr. Her father, Robin Sr. was a cigar aficionado. So young Robin learned she could gain her father's approval by smoking cigars. She played pee-wee hockey much to her father's delight.

Their relationship broke down when Robin, an obviously beautiful girl, started liking boys. The few times that she talks with her father, his disappointment is obvious and their broken relationship is real enough to depart from the show's main goal to make us laugh. He has never gotten over his disappointment with her being a girl.

Most Christian parents would not act like the fictional Robin Scherbatsky father. But Christian parents are principled parents. They have value systems usually connected to strong opinions. These value systems do influence their future hopes for their children.

Growing in Your Objectivity
Seven Questions

It may be obvious why you are disappointed. Your child has robbed a bank and is being sentenced to 20 years in prison. Your disappointment is warranted. But when your child is normal they will probably go through the process of three steps forward and one step back. Having an objective view of your child's progress in growing toward strong Christian beliefs will help you be avoid disappointment.

Answer the following questions honestly.
1. Why am I disappointed with my child?
2. Is my disappointment appropriate?
3. What are my undefined expectations?
4. Should I lower or change my expectations?
5. Am I withholding my love because of my disappointment?
6. Have I explained to my child that I love them but cannot approve of their present path?
7. Can I give approval to something they are doing while not approving other things?

Approval and Disapproval

Adult children still need appropriate love and support from their parents. Without admitting this need for your support they may push to have your approval in areas that they know you disapprove. An objective Christian parent's belief in God's values should guide their approval or disapproval of all human actions. Biblical values do not change because your child has decided to walk another path. Your child's present justifications or struggles with your values should not affect your approval or disapproval.

The Pain of Disappointment

When talking with your child explain that you cannot GIVE your approval, without really approving.

If you approve, you approve.

If you are neutral, you are neutral.

If you disapprove, you disapprove.

But your disapproval does not mean that you do not love them. In fact your sense of disappointment is rooted in your deep love for them. You will always be supportive when they are going the right direction. You love them, no matter what direction they are going. You will always believe in their potential to accomplish many things.

Your Mission - If You Wish to Accept It

Correction helps change a person's direction in life.
Encouragement strengthens a person on their present path.

Your mission as a parent of an adult is to, whenever possible, encourage. Unperceived disappointment paralyzes our ability to encourage. It can make us conflicted and confused.

You do not have to voice your disappointment. Simply remain silent, when you can't encourage. The bigger your dreams the more potential there is for discouragement. The only relationship that has no potential for disappointment is the one where the bar is set very low. Don't let your disappointment take away your positive expectations.

Keep dreaming big for your kids. Keep the bar high and encourage them to succeed before God and man.

7

The Loss of What Use to Be
Seven Steps of Transition

When our first child was 4 years old, Michelle and I moved to 15 acres in the foothills of the Tehachapi Mountains in California. We bought a double wide mobile home and had our "Little Mobile Home on the Prairie." I worked and we sacrificed so Michelle could stay home and home school the girls.

Michelle and I loved this time of our life. We loved having kids. We loved raising our kids. Some of the happiest times of our lives were those times on our 15 acres. Our memories are filled with cold nights around the pot belly stove; snow storms; hot summers in our homemade pool; the special times with our little family.

It hit me one Thanksgiving Day as I drove by a large house with 10 to 15 cars parked neatly in front. There were many family gatherings going on in our neighborhood; families celebrating together with friends. My emotions were mixed about the day's events, since my relationship had been strained with one of my adult children and only half of our kids would be there that Thanksgiving.

It hit me that day, as I drove by that house, with so many cars. The group of 6 people who had lived together; celebrated holidays together; taken vacations together, was no more. That group of 6 people that was known as the Grinsteads, had morphed into six adults, two grandkids and two spouses. That happy little family was gone. Those special times that had brought Michelle and me so much joy was gone, forever.

I suppose there have been many books written on the *Empty Nest Syndrome*. But as a man, I assumed they were written mainly from the mother's point of view. I had not thought of our family as "A Nest" I have never read any of them. Our lives had been full of many people and duties; full of crises and heartaches.

The Loss of What Use to Be

As each child left and started their new adult life, I would joke that this had been our goal. We had been working toward the goal of our children growing up and having enough courage, strength and intelligence to be on their own. I was very thankful that my kids were leaving and were full of hope about their futures.

As they left, one at a time, Michelle and I had more free time, freedom to do things that were postponed while we had small children. There were immediate benefits from the kids growing up and we were experiencing positive things from our "Empty Nest."

Michelle would cry, as they drove away to their new homes and then we would get back to life. The house would become a little quieter and a lot cleaner. Our hearts were not filled with sorrow or turmoil, but faith and encouragement. A little quieter was not a bad thing and although Michelle cried, we were happy.

But now 6 years later, it hit me, hard. We had enjoyed life together as a close knit family from 1975 to 2005, thirty years. My role of caretaker, caregiver, and supplier of the necessities of small human beings was coming to an end. The children were all gone, all grown up. They had very quickly formed different families, all in different stages of life.

The irony of this predicament is that because my wife and I had worked very hard, sacrificing and doing things for the good of the whole family, the loss was greater. If we had not put off buying that convertible and bought the van (actually two vans); if we had not sacrificed so that one of us could stay home and raise our kids; if we had been less committed to our family the loss would have been less. Now the void was huge, because our family had been one of the main things of our lives.

That Thanksgiving Day I began processing what was obvious. The one thing that I had worked so hard for; sacrificed so long for was gone. It would not be back. There would be other relationships and other joys, but Greg and Michelle Grinstead and the four kids were no more.

I suppose the steps that are taken to process this loss are different for each person. Other losses such as divorce or premature death of a loved one, I am sure would hit harder and last longer.

But for those of us who tried hard to do right by our kids (I assume this is most parents); for those of us who tried hard and succeeded a little; who had a loving home; we need to process the loss of this wonderful thing we had for decades; a family.

7 Steps of Transition

1. Contemplate this dichotomy.
   A. I want my kids to grow up and do well without me.
   B. I really miss the times of closeness and fun with my children.

2. Process your regrets. It is normal to have regrets.
   A. Write down your thoughts.
   B. Talk about your regrets and what you wished you had done differently.
   C. Write your kids a letter (don't send it, if it would be hurtful to them).
   D. Ask for forgiveness from God and your children.

3. Begin to let the past be the past by not dwelling upon the things that can never be changed. Once you have taken time to contemplate your emotions, begin to redirect your thoughts. Let your mind be filled with positive things about life and the future.

4. Find new relationships that matter. Give yourself time and energy to develop new relationships and don't force it. Your family became close naturally as life unfolded. Let new relationships also develop as life unfolds.

5. If you are still married, this is the time to do things with your spouse. Be spontaneous and do simple things together. Develop a schedule of doing things enjoyable together. Plan special times together and take time for each other.

6. Keep a sense of purpose and calling. Don't be tricked into thinking that doing nothing will bring happiness or fulfillment. God has purpose for you. Find it and finish your course well.

7. Finally, don't force your adult children by guilt or manipulation to stay in a forced "happy family." Let new family relationships develop naturally as each adult chooses the path they want to walk. Give your kids the freedom to not be with you, while reassuring them that you love them.

My family, full of needy small children is gone. But God has new things ahead for me.

> "Do not call to mind the former things,
> Or ponder things of the past.
>
> "Behold, I will do something new,
> Now it will spring forth;
> Will you not be aware of it?
>
> "I will even make a roadway in the wilderness,
> Rivers in the desert."
> *Isaiah 43:18-19 NASB*

PART II

This section addresses the problems that arise between parents and their adult children. You can have great kids and be a great parent of smaller children and still need help from some of the chapters in this section.

We all look around and see happy families that seem to be closer and less troubled. But the Bible is full of families that are troubled. From Adam and his son murdering the other, to King David's son leading a rebellion to take the Kingdom from him, the Bible is full of broken, sinful adult children and their suffering parents.

John Maxwell is a respected Christian leader. In his bestselling book, *The 15 Invaluable Laws of Growth*, he is candid about his own transition to being a parent of adults. In Chapter 4, *The Law of Reflection*, he uses himself as an example of how to reflect.

He states in his list of "Personal Awareness Questions:"

3. What is My Highest High?
Without a doubt, my family is the source of the highest highs in my life. Margaret is my best friend. I cannot imagine life without her. And we are enjoying our favorite season of life now as grandparents.

4. What is My Lowest Low?
Ironically, my lowest lows have also come as the result of family. Why? Because I love my family members so much, yet I have to let them make their own choices. That can be tough for someone with my personality....

May this section help you with the complex questions that arise as you try to have the best relationship that you can have with your adult child.

8

When You Are Deeply Troubled

Relieving the Pressure of Strained Relationships

Almost all parents want to have good relationships with their adult children. We would love to be close to our children and their children. We would like to be more than a convenient babysitter or a place that they visit every other Christmas.

Some of the highest joys and deepest pains come from our relationships to our adult children. Our concerns grow in intensity from their first day of Kindergarten, to their leaving for college. No matter how emotionally prepared or mature they are the pitfalls of growing from late adolescent to adulthood are many.

Now they are on their own, sort of. They are making all their decisions without input from you or anyone you would recommend. They are sorting out what they believe and why they believe it. They do not seem to be learning from their many mistakes, as quickly as you would like. They continue to repeat bad choices from faulty thinking month after month.

You have prayed and prayed with seeming little heavenly help. You want to believe and you know God is good, but.... You are deeply troubled about your child.

Some of the Pressure Is Coming From You

When you find your mind coming back to your children's problems over and over again, turn to the most important relationship in your life; your relationship with God. Become aware that YOU are having a problem, not just your child and ask for His help.

If you have neglected your relationship with God, recommit to a daily interaction with Him. When you are at your lowest, turn your heart toward God and have a conversation. Focus on the one who has the answers, instead of those who need answers. In our deepest times of need, our small heart movements toward God bring a large response from Him.

Obsess About the Right Things

Jill Briscoe, a bestselling author and highly regarded Christian speaker, relates in her book *The Deep Place Where Nobody Goes: Conversations with God on the Steps of My Soul.* Page 142

"Why do I worry so much? Looking back on nearly 70 years of worrying (my mother tells me I was a worried baby!), I am ashamed at my much worrying…."

God shows Jill it is OK to look at the problem, from every angle, each day and pray about it one time. Just as the Children of Israel walked around Jericho, one time each day, she could think about and pray about the present problem, one time. Then give the battle to God. She should stop giving herself permission to worry about it any longer that day.

Once a day think about what you can do. Think about what you should have done. Think about what you are going to do. Once a day think about and talk about the problem that is on your mind. Then let God take that thing that you are worrying about. This is the principle in Philippians 4:6-8.

Be anxious for nothing, but in everything by prayer and supplication with thanksgiving let your requests be made known to God. And the peace of God, which surpasses all comprehension, will guard your hearts and your minds in Christ Jesus.

Finally, brethren, whatever is true, whatever is honorable, whatever is right, whatever is pure, whatever is lovely, whatever is of good repute, if there is any excellence and if anything worthy of praise, **dwell on these things**. *Philippians 4:6-8 NASB*

Think about the things that are true and honorable and right and pure and beautiful and respected. *Philippians 4:8b NCV*

Medicate on the fact that God is on your side as you pray for your adult child's wellbeing. God knows your heart's condition. He has not left you or forsaken you. Memorize the scripture above.

"Let not your heart be troubled; you believe in God, believe also in Me. *Jesus speaking in John 14:1*

Peace I leave with you, my peace I give to you; not as the world gives do I give to you. Let not your heart be troubled, neither let it be afraid. *Jesus speaking in John 14:27*

The Holy Spirit is with us to give us comfort. The Holy Spirit's comfort does not numb us or minimize the seriousness of the problem. God comforts us by strengthening our heart's trust in His power, wisdom and authority. Although the problems may be serious, He is big enough to deal with them. He is wise enough to bring a just outcome. He is strong enough to deliver and rescue.

Do the Things That Bring Healing
Avoid Everything Else

Late one night, when I was closing up the church, I turned off the sanctuary lights. I grabbed something from the platform and since it was completely dark, I tripped over the monitor speakers on the floor, twisting my knee. I wore a brace on that knee for several months. The healing process of a strained joint starts with taking the pressure off the joint.

Identify the area of strain in your relationship with your child and avoid putting any pressure on it. Be positive and supportive, whenever possible. Make an effort to reconcile without addressing everything at once. Let God work on the problem areas, as you give Him the space to work.

> Never pay back evil for evil to anyone. Respect what is right in the sight of all men. If possible, so far as it depends on you, be at peace with all men. Never take your own revenge, beloved, but leave room for the wrath of God, for it is written, "VENGEANCE IS MINE, I WILL REPAY," says the Lord. *Romans 12:17-19*

Before the relationship is strained to the point of fully breaking, take steps to do what you can do to live in peace with your adult child. "If possible, so far as it depends on you, be at peace."

If your child reacts to negative comments, be positive.
If your child reacts when you talk about the past, stop talking about the past.

If possible, as far as it concerns you, release the stress. There will be time to address the issues at hand. Work toward the time when these issues can be dealt with in a constructive way. By both you and your child agreeing to consider each other's position.

Open a Dialogue for Reconciliation

If there is an openness to talk, talk. But set the following goals for any strained conversation. There may be an openness to receive correction later. There may be another time to "Get truth out..." Don't try to win an argument. Don't try to change their value system.

Goal # 1

You just want to talk to help your child understand, process and be set free from the effect of your past failures. Ask for forgiveness.

Goal # 2

You just want to talk so that you can have as good of a relationship that is possible with your child.

There are many reasons why people who have stressed relationships want to talk. Sometimes talking can make things worse. If an adult just wants to vent or accuse to cause others pain, it is probably better to avoid talking. The above goals can keep a discussion on track.

You can choose not to participate in painful, unproductive discussions by asking for a clarification about why something is being stated. Is the goal to have a better relationship?

Humbly Ask for Forgiveness

Ask for forgiveness if it is appropriate. Chapter 4 goes into detail about when and how to share your failures. Your humble requests for forgiveness may or may not be accepted, but ask anyway.

Gently and softly reject any false accusations or deceptions coming from your child having a warped view of reality. Many of life's failures and difficulties are hidden from your kids as they are growing up. They do not need to know the details of the events that happened when they were younger.

It may be time for you to fill in the blanks for them. As an adult they may be able to understand what caused some of the failures that you are asking them to forgive. If you perceive that sharing these details is creating a bigger gap, stop and rethink your approach.

Your child may have to experience more of life to understand. They may also view your sharing of other's failures as your blaming others for your shortcomings. Honoring and respecting your spouse may require you to avoid or just not talk about certain things that have happened. Adultery and other serious failures should be treated as confidences only to be revealed with permission.

When you talk, you will probably disagree about what really happened. This is normal and you should not get upset about these distorted memories. Your child remembers events from an immature child's perspective. Now they are adults and may be ready to rethink their young judgments of past events.

If you disagree about the facts of an event, be gentle and clear. Don't use harsh pronouncements that may make it seem you are rejecting your child. Reject the faulty memory by saying, "That is not my adult perception of that event," and then say why.

My Wife and My Prayer for God's Help
When We Are Deeply Troubled

Dear God, help us in our weaknesses and bring us to renewed faith. We are at times fainthearted. Meet us in our weakness and strengthen us with the power of the Holy Spirit. Come into this situation with our children and work your will. Accomplish your good intentions quickly and keep our children from evil.

God, bring your supernatural power into their lives. Give us wisdom to know how to react and when to speak and when to not say anything. Help us be a part of the answer in this time of our children's lives. We ask these things with full knowledge of your deep love for our children. We ask these things knowing you want to help.

We pray again, today and commit our children into your hand for your keeping. Thank you, God. Amen.

9

When They Don't Want To Have Anything to Do with You
Healing Broken Relationships

J esus told them this story: "A man had two sons. The younger son told his father, 'I want my share of your estate now before you die.' So his father agreed to divide his wealth between his sons.

"A few days later this younger son packed all his belongings and moved to a distant land, and there he wasted all his money in wild living. About the time his money ran out, a great famine swept over the land, and he began to starve. He persuaded a local farmer to hire him, and the man sent him into his fields to feed the pigs. The young man became so hungry that even the pods he was feeding the pigs looked good to him. But no one gave him anything.

"When he finally came to his senses, he said to himself, 'At home even the hired servants have food enough to spare, and here I am dying of hunger! I will go home to my father and say, "Father, I have sinned against both heaven and you, and I am no longer worthy of being called your son. Please take me on as a hired servant.'"

"So he returned home to his father. And while he was still a long way off, his father saw him coming. Filled with love and compassion, he ran to his son, embraced him, and kissed him. His son said to him, 'Father, I have sinned against both heaven and you, and I am no longer worthy of being called your son.

"But his father said to the servants, 'Quick! Bring the finest robe in the house and put it on him. Get a ring for his finger and sandals for his feet. And kill the calf we have been fattening. We must celebrate with a feast, for this son of mine was dead and has now returned to life. He was lost, but now he is found.' So the party began... *Luke 15:11-22 NLV*

When we read this story, it is Jesus' intent for the father to represent God and the prodigal son to represent most of us humans who so easily go astray and need to return and repent. This is the third of three stories that are recorded in Luke 15 about the lost being found. Jesus' main intent is easy to understand. Most of us relate to the story from the wayward son's point of view.

But now that you are a parent of adult who wants to have nothing, or very little to do with you, the father's perspective is insightful. This story gives us a small glimpse of God's "Loving Father Heart" toward all of His children. As parents, we can also relate to the great sadness and loss that the father felt when his son left. The continuing pain that the father felt as the broken relationship continued over a long time period.

We don't know how many sleepless nights the father spent praying for and wondering about his "lost son." Finally the father wondered whether his son was dead. We can assume that the prodigal had had no communication with his father for the whole time that he had been gone.

In today's terms, the son had not returned the father's text messages, voice mails or replied to his emails. The son had stopped being his father's "friend" on Face Book. We don't know what the prodigal's complaints were in the relationship. But it is obvious that the relationship was completely broken.

The love that the father shows the returning son reveals God's deep concern and strong love that rises above the pain of the separation. Anyone who has had a child completely break relationship can relate to the great joy that the father felt when he saw his son, in the distance.

The Pain Caused by the Prodigal

When I was in my twenties, I decided to build a two story garage on a slab of concrete in the back yard that the previous owner had poured and then abandoned. The driveway came from the street to the slab and so I bought a book and proceeded to build the garage from the treated bottom plates to the tongue and grove one inch plywood on the second story floor joists.

Since no one in my family had been a carpenter, I read the book and built the garage. I built the whole building with box nails, not the sinkers an experienced carpenter would use. My wife, Michelle was standing on a step ladder on the 2nd floor and holding a 16 foot long, wobbly roof joist. I grabbed my heavy framing hammer to nail the joist into place. I bent several of the box nails in my inexperience. So I decided to use more strength and hit the next nail as hard as I could. I hit my thumb instead.

The pain shot up my hand to my shoulder. I had never felt physical pain this intense. It was weeks before I went back up on the 2nd floor and finished the project (with sinker nails). And I have never hit my thumb with a hammer again. Four decades later the lesson of the framing hammer and the nail is seared into my mind, and when I have a hammer in my hand, I position all my fingers correctly and take special care with my swing.

Some parent child relationships will bring a similar response after a unforeseen argument. "I shouldn't do that again." Or after being confronted as the prodigal did his father, we can react normally. "That was the worst emotional pain I have ever experienced."

Even when you and your child want a good relationship, you are programmed to not "hit your thumb" again. You begin to wonder why you no longer want to be around your child and you feel guilty. You try to avoid the area that caused the pain and continue to relate but then something else happens. And you "hit your thumb" again.

Intense and Conflicting Emotions

Shame or guilt – "What did I do to cause this?"
Self-pity – "I didn't do anything to cause this!"
Resentment – "This is not right. I should not be treated this way."

This pattern of experiencing intense emotions, then trying again can continue for decades with no one addressing the underlying cause. Parents do what any sane person would do. They avoid their adult children. Here is a list of Pains that you may have experienced that may be causing you to avoid your adult children.

1. The Pain of "not feeling welcome" in their home. (Rejection)
2. The Pain of being mocked in things that are important to you. (Dishonored)
3. The Pain of feeling that what you feel does not matter. (Disrespected)
4. The Pain of feeling that you are not important or needed. (Diminished)
5. The Pain that your child is immoral in their lifestyle. (You are a failure)

Guarding Against Self-Pity

Normal conflict between teenagers and parents is painful but your teen is still in the home. The hope of helping them is alive. But in the case of the Prodigal Son, helplessness can lead to desperation. He leaves and never looks back.

"After all the times you have sacrificed;
"After all the years that your own needs went unfulfilled for your child's welfare;
"After all the decisions that were made with only your child's welfare in mind;
"After all the times of love and nurture, they break all ties. Why?"

Find Your Love Again

Elie Wiesel once said that the opposite of love is not hate. It is indifference. This indifference can be the end result of continuing in a painful relationship. It is because we love our children that we are not complacent. We may have to overcome resentment, anger or fear as we continue to love. But indifference effects your motives to keep seeking a good relationship.

After a few years of "hitting our thumbs," our tendency is to not just avoid the pain but to become complacent. After a few years of your child not coming to holiday dinners, not calling, not caring, the pain can lead to a disconnection that looks like indifference.

The Prodigal Daughter

Doris was 36 years old. She had been a rebellious teenager and had married her first husband young. He abused her and he went to prison. Doris's parents loved her and paid for her counseling after her first marriage broke up.

She moved back into her parent's home at the time of her younger sister's high school graduation. She arranged to have her sister move out with her the week after graduation.

Years later Doris and her sister totally cut their parents off. They moved and would not give their addresses to them, in case they wanted to send her a card. At first, her parents were in confusion. Then they became emotionally hurt and finally they became complacent. Her loving parents had never been overly controlling or selfishly distant from their children. I talked with them in their third year of exile.

They had found some solace from their negative feelings by becoming indifferent. They tried to cut their daughters off emotionally the way they would other adults. But since they could not distance themselves from their parental emotions fully, they were still tormented. They were stuck.

The Answer for Doris' Parents

The answer is not to become emotionally numb. When you become numb, it can affect all of your other relationships. The answer is to find the love that you had for your child when they were babies. The answer is to rise above your normal adult to adult emotions.

When your children were very young, you had no expectations of them and no control over anything that they did. But you loved them. You loved them no matter how big a mess they made. You loved them no matter how slow they were at learning to not make some of those messes in their pants. You loved them because you were their parents and they needed you.

Now they are adults, and you can't control anything they do. Now they have cut you off and you cannot have any expectations of their behavior changing. But they are still your children. You still want the best for them.

In all human relationships, you have boundaries and expectations. In most human relationships, you are free to decide to go your separate ways. As your children grew up your expectations of their behavior toward you and others increased incrementally until you were putting the same expectations upon them as other adults.

But now you find yourself with no control over your child's behavior and no ability to expect a change. But this is your child and they will always be your child. You will always be their parent. This is one relationship that will remain whether anyone wants it.

Decide to Love Your Prodigal Child

Decide to be a loving parent to your prodigal child, by loving them the way you loved them when they were a baby. Love them without any assurances that the circumstances will change, the way the Prodigal Son's father must have reacted.

Your baby was not there to make YOU happy. Because the baby brought a lot of joy to the family did not mean that that was the baby's job. The baby was not there to do anything for you. You were there to do something for them. Now the baby is an adult and it would seem that they no longer need anything from you.

You can love your child with that special parental love tweaked just a bit. Love them and pray for them expecting nothing in return. The only expectation that you have is that IF they come to their senses, they will repent. To have a relationship that is improving there needs to be repentance for past bad behavior.

Doris and her sister's decision to isolate themselves from their loving parents allowed their parents to avoid reoccurring painful experiences and love them from a distance.

It was best that Doris' parents would become realists. The relationship is not good. The relationship is not strained or tense. The relationship is broken. But they can still love her.

Separate Them from Their Behavior

View your child as a struggling, sometimes weak person like you; imprisoned by their wrong thinking or bad behavior.

View their behavior and their actions as wrong. Their actions are bad. You do not love or even like their wrong actions.

Your response to your child's behavior can be different from your response to your child. In Christian terms, this is similar to, "Loving the sinner and hating the sin."

You can decide to love your child the way you use to love your child when they were small. Not expecting anything in return. You are there to help when it is appropriate. You will love them no matter how they treat you.

You should hate the sinful behavior. Since you love your child and wish them the best, you hate their wrong behavior even more. There are consequences to immoral actions. You should pray they would come to their senses as soon as possible and repent.

Did the Devil Make Them Do It?

... so that no advantage would be taken of us by Satan, for we are not ignorant of his schemes. *II Corinthians 2:11 NASB*

The problems in human dynamics are divided unevenly between several areas. These areas are intertwined and overlapping but when identified as separate can bring clarity to your understanding of your child's bad behavior.

Your child's physical condition (brain chemistry)
Your child's thoughts and wrong ideas (value system)
Your child's feelings and mistaken emotions (sinful heart)
Your child's heart and spiritual condition (need of deliverance)

Finally, be strong in the Lord and in the strength of His might. Put on the full armor of God, so that you will be able to stand firm against the schemes of the devil.

For our struggle is not against flesh and blood, but against the rulers, against the powers, against the world forces of this darkness, against the spiritual forces of wickedness in the heavenly places.

Therefore, take up the full armor of God, so that you will be able to resist in the evil day, and having done everything, to stand firm.
Ephesians 6:10-13 NASB

There is an unseen battle raging that can be won with the authority of heaven. Wrong behavior and wrong thinking can cause your child to become spiritually oppressed. You have the spiritual authority in the unseen realms described in Chapter 3.

This approach does not excuse your child of their responsibility to do the right thing and repent and ask for forgiveness for hurting others. But a Christian view of bad behavior encompasses all of these areas.

Leave the Door Open
Open Ended "I Love You"

A person who pursues an unwanted relationship with another adult can have a restraining order issued against them. The father in the story of the Prodigal did not chase his son from place to place. We also should give our children the amount of space that they are requesting. Giving God the space to work within their hearts, can be more effective that badgering them. Leave the door open.

"I will always love you and I want to have a good relationship with you, when you decide you desire it too." Occasionally express declarations of your love toward your child, no matter how bad the relationship.

When possible continue to include the prodigal in your gift giving. Birthday presents, Christmas presents, even gifts given unexpectedly can be done as an action of leaving the door open. Do not make your children earn their gifts. A gift earned is not a gift because it was not freely given.

Fill the Vacuum

God has a great plan for you in the final seasons of your life. Don't allow offense, pride, unforgiveness from unwarranted attacks stop you from finishing the course well. Don't get stuck on your adult child's bad behavior. Decide to have the Apostle Paul's testimony at the end of your life.

I have fought the good fight,
I have finished the course,
I have kept the faith;
II Timothy 4:7 NASB

Don't become distracted or emotionally disabled so that you neglect helping the other people who need you. Be like Joseph in the Dungeon, and keep the faith, knowing that in the proper time, God can bring about justice.

Rehearse these truths.

For I consider that the sufferings of this present time are not worthy to be compared with the glory that is to be revealed to us.
Romans 8:18 NASB

And we know that God causes all things to work together for good to those who love God,
to those who are called according to His purpose.
Romans 8:28 NASB

But in all these things we overwhelmingly conquer through Him who loved us.
Romans 8:37 NASB

10

When They Don't Listen to You
Listen to Them

Listen to your father who begot you,
And do not despise your mother when she is old.
Proverbs 23:22

W hen my children were young, I would share the, "When I was your age stories." Parenting books encouraged me to talk with my children about when I was a child. I think that was great advice and I wouldn't do anything differently.

When my children were pre-teens and teens, I would instruct them about practical matters and life in general. I viewed my job as a parent as helping my children to avoid the mistakes I had made, by talking about my mistakes. I talked about car maintenance, electric bills, working hard and anything else that came up. I talked and they seemed to be listening. They were my captive audience and it was my job to instruct and their job to learn. I wouldn't do anything differently.

The years have gone and I no longer need to be the wise one with all the answers. In this season of my life, I have a few things to say that are valuable. I have learned not to speak when I do not know what I am talking about. I have grown a little wiser.

Why can't my kids see that I am wiser now than before?

Problem Number One
They Think They Already Know

They think that they know what I am going to say before I say it. The curse of being a good parent is that you have repeated yourself a lot. This is the reason that some parents who were not repeating themselves, as they should have, are now being listened to more.

My children have been gone for several years and they think that I have stopped growing in wisdom. They think that what I believe, I have believed for years. They think that I have nothing new to say.

The Solution: Start saying things like, "I don't believe that way anymore." Or "My views on that have changed." Then don't volunteer anything more. Make them curious and require them to ask for your views on specific issues.

Problem Number Two
They Have Found Other "Experts"

Your children now have other "Experts" in their lives. Your children have broken adults, who love the openness of young adults and see an opportunity to be the smartest person in the room. These foolish counselors become new experts and pronounce platitudes that sound like wisdom to your still maturing children.

These people are unaware why they gravitate to giving advice to the newly independent young adult. They do not see that their ideas are only new to the newly independent. When spouting their platitudes that seem like new ideas, their views are not challenged. They like the place of importance and draw little groups of twenty somethings around themselves for something called "Christian fellowship."

These older adults may be college teachers, professors or just someone in church. They also may be young leaders the same age as your child, whose ideas have not been tested. Young people love "new" ideas and can be easily deceived.

> ...there is nothing new under the sun
> *Ecclesiastes 1:9b NASB*

Unless younger children learn the basic truth of Ecclesiastes 1:9 they can easily reject your view for a "new" view. A large percentage of things learned in your twenties are "New to you." It might be an old truth from the Bible, but it is "New to you." This leaves your children open to old deceptions parading as the latest hot topic.

Besides their peers and other people masquerading as wise sages, there is the internet. From Yahoo News to Google, every imaginable deception, lie and twisted fact can be found within seconds. Without Biblical based thinking and good discernment, confusion leads to deception.

Problem Number Three
You Have Been Replaced by Good Counselors

Your children now have legitimate and good counselors. Your place of the one that had the last word has others input now. Independence means having the freedom to listen to others. This transition should have started in your child's teen years. Teen group leaders and their pastor hopefully gained input as they questioned their value system.

Take a step back and allow your children the freedom to listen to and discern other leader's ideas.

Problem Number Four
Knowledge Has Increased

Your children probably know more than you when reviewing their world. In today's fast changing world, knowledge is increasing exponentially. Knowledge is also becoming more and more specialized. Assuming that you have become successful, you will also have increased in the specialized knowledge of your field. You have gained knowledge about one thing at the expense of another. Language, manners, phones, computer programs are quickly changing.

I would encourage you to stay up-to-date on the culture as much as possible. Not because of your children, but because of their children. Trying to remain hip by knowing the latest movie star is a lesson in futility. But remaining able to relate to the world your grandkids live in is a noble endeavor.

There is a plus to being involved in the fast changing world of your grandkids. Teenagers create new language and different cultural norms to be different from their parents. Many resent their parents "butting in" to this new culture. But your grandkids will probably welcome you into their culture as someone who is taking an interest in their lives.

Problem Number Five
You Are Just Trying to Help

My wife and I developed the "Maria Barone" rule when visiting our kid's homes and relating into their world. What is the "Marie Barone" rule? *"No negative statements or comments of any kind, For any reason, at any time."*

The beginning scene of Everybody Loves Raymond, Season 9, Episode 3:

Raymond is trying to hurry everyone out of his house, because he is planning on having an amorous night with his wife, Debra. His brother, Robert, wants to stay but reluctantly goes. Raymond's mother Marie, Robert and His father are all going out the open front door when Marie turns to his wife and says:

"Oh Debra, I would like to take the boys to that Happy Zone tomorrow, if that is OK with you?"
Debra (excited and happy) "Oh that would be great, thank you Marie."
Marie (turning to leave) "And while we are out, I will just get them haircuts, (under her breath) OK?"
Debra "Oh wait - they don't need haircuts."
Marie (turning back to Debra in a sweet voice) "Oh but they do. Maybe you haven't noticed, but the boys look at little (thinking for the right word) slovenly lately."
Audience laughs.
Debra (with Raymond standing behind her apprehensively- knowing this could sidetrack his plans.) (Debra drawing back) "Excuse Me"

When They Don't Listen to You

Raymond (looking worried) "Oh no."
Audience laughs.
Robert – Raymond's brother, comes back into the view of the audience, now interested in how Raymond's night is about to get sidetracked.
Audience laughs.
Marie looks directly at Debra with an innocent look, (implying she doesn't understand Debra's reaction)
Debra indignantly "What are you saying, Marie, that my kids look like (pauses) Hobos?"
Marie (smiling) "Heavens no, Hobos have beards."
Audience laughs.
Debra (looking down and then shaking her head from side to side, with her hands on her hips, with a look of frustration) "I hate when you do this Marie!"
Marie (with a look of concern and feigning innocence) says, "Do what dear? Help?"
Audience laughs.
Raymond – as he moves around his wife to get between his mother and wife. (Smiling) "Yes, that is all she is doing. She is just helping. Well, good night, helpful mommy"
Audience laughs
Debra gently pushes Raymond out of her way "Marie, why can't you just be direct with me?"
Marie "Well I'm sorry (pauses, thinking) but it is hard to be direct, with someone who jumps down your throat every time you make a helpful suggestion." (Raymond grimaces, Robert looks happy)
Marie "There, is that direct enough?"
Audience laughs
Debra (crossing her arms) "You know what Marie, I'll take the boys to the Happy Zone, and I'll take care of their haircuts and I'll do it all without you."
Marie (smiling) "That is fine with me dear -at least you're finally doing something about it."
Marie turns and leaves.

Debra picks something up and storms toward the kitchen, as Raymond stands there wondering how things could go bad so fast. Robert, his brother gloats over his misfortune.

For those who haven't watched the program, the audience laughs quickly because they all know these characters. They know that anytime Raymond's mom, Marie Barone comes to Ray's house, she says something negative about something. She tries to help by criticizing Debra's cooking, Debra's cleaning; She has negative observations about how Debra disciplines the kids. She is always amazed that her "help" is rejected.

Negative speech can easily become a habit. My wife and I made the "Marie Barone" rule when we found ourselves just trying to help. We would visit our kid's homes and immediately see several items that could be fixed, changed or well "helped with."

When the rule was first instituted, my wife was amazed at how many times she had to stop herself from saying something negative. She had not been aware of how negative she had become. She was just trying to help.

Problem Number 6
They See the Dirt That Is Missed

My wife's janitorial company use to clean carpets in a large Los Angeles County facility. The carpet cleaners were amazed at how much dirt would come out of the carpet. The water in the extractor would literally be black. Unfortunately, her clients never saw the black water. They only would see the spots of dirt that remained.

The same would happen to the other custodians. Their training included a quick scan of the area for obvious things that were missed before leaving an area. You would think that after spending 30 minutes cleaning, they would not leave something obviously wrong. They saw all the dirt they removed and were not focused on the dirt that they left.

Of course the client would call and complain about the items that were obviously not done.

When talking about your past family life with your child this lesson is valuable. Your child, if normal will focus on the dirt that you left. They will not comprehend all the dirt you removed. You can try to tell them about the decades you have watched, worked, sacrificed, but they will focus on the few problems.

In many cases the few problems have been exaggerated in your child's adult mind by their childish memories. Clueless friends or counselors may have encouraged these exaggeration and distortions of past problems.

So how do your proceed without sounding like you are minimizing their painful memory? Ask for forgiveness for anything that was perceived as a failure whenever possible. Don't let a lie's power to imprison, continue without being confronted. If your child has the facts wrong, gently, quietly correct them. But if there is a small amount of truth in what they are saying, ask for forgiveness. Don't let the fact that most of your actions were right stop you from acknowledging when they were wrong.

Most parents don't like to talk about their past sacrifices and acts of love. Most parents don't like to talk about the many things that they automatically did for their children's benefit. They went without because they loved their kids. They put up with all kinds of things, because it was the best thing for their kids.

Parents don't want to come across as someone who is asking for credit or thanks. They don't want to come across as someone who wouldn't do it all over again. So they remain quiet about all the dirt that was removed, leaving their adult children partially deceived.

To correct this, take regular times at small family events to talk about "the dirt that was removed." An easy way to do this (that does not appear self-serving) is to write out a thank you note to your spouse. Compliment your spouse on the hard sacrifices that were made.

Write a tribute and talk about the time when mom went without to give everyone a good Christmas…. Tell family stories that review the past from an adult's perspective. Your child may begin to see the mountains of work that was done for their benefit with their adult mind.

By regularly honoring those who sacrificed in front of your adult child you may break inaccurate conclusions. You will be doing something noble. You will be helping your child learn to obey God's moral laws of right and wrong – The Fifth Commandment. They will be able to see that there is a lot to honor their mother and their father for.

Three Reactions to Your Advice

All adults experience the following three reactions to their parents at one time in their lives.
1. Those that cannot listen or hear their parent's advice.
2. Those that hear and still have to learn by trying other options.
3. Those that listen and avoid the pitfalls of the past.

1. Those That Cannot Hear

The fact that they are not listening now may be a phase that they are growing through. They may want their independence and not listening is the easiest action that they can take to appear independent. When they mature, they will realize that they can remain independent and still hear those around them that have wise advice.

In the adult world, unsolicited or unwanted advice is not welcomed, even if it is given with good intentions. The person who walks through life, giving everyone advice can be viewed as a know it all. Your child may just be asking for the same respect that other adults give one another. "Please offer your advice when it is requested."

If you have an adult child that won't listen, then learn to be quiet. Occasionally, carefully plant seeds of wisdom. Don't make pronouncements that are directives, statements of authority, or off handed remarks. Learn to be a seed planter. With prayer and a few hard knocks, your child could quickly change their attitude.

2. Those That Hear But Don't Follow Through

If your adult child hears you and agrees with you and then tries another path anyway, keep the lines of communication open. Don't be offended. Don't accuse them of dishonoring you. Don't accuse them of being immature, because they have not followed through. It might be childishness or it might be an adult exercising their independence.

Independent adults set their own priorities. Since time and energy is finite, we all do not get around to doing some things. They may be agreeing that your suggestions are true but setting different priorities. Time will tell, if the thing they neglect is the most important.

When dealing with complicated life situations, even when trying to do the right thing, there may be several "right" ways of proceeding. Let them process life differently than you.

It took you time to grow in wisdom. It will probably take them time too. We all learn from what doesn't work as from what does work. One of the definitions of an emotionally mature adult would be someone who can learn from their mistakes and find success. So, relax, pray and yes, continue to share your advice. They are listening.

3. Those That Hear and Act

If you have a child that listens, and avoids the pitfalls of life, rejoice. You are blessed. If your child's spouse also responds with, "That's a really good idea," you are doubly blessed.

If you have influence in your child's life in this way, treasure it and protect it. Don't over use it. Hold your piece until the important issues come up. In real world situations, there are usually 4 right and 10 wrong answers. Let your child pick a few wrong answers and hold your peace. Cherish that your child values your input and respects your wisdom.

Make Your Advice a Thing to Be Treasured
Instead of Avoided

God will give you creative ways to help your adult children, when they are trying to learn how to honor you but do not want to listen to you.

1. Make a You-Tube video for your family and talk from your heart to each person and send it on a holiday.
2. Be positive. 80% positive, 20% negative and no more; advice coming from a wounded or bitter person is hard to accept.
3. Start a tradition of talking about important stuff at a special time of year. On Thanksgiving Day, take your son out while the women are cooking or vice versa.
4. Write one page of your thoughts about yourself, your wife, or your kids. Send it on Father's Day, Veterans Day, or Memorial Day.
5. Avoid giving public advice at large family gatherings and parties. Use these times to talk small talk and have fun, keeping the lines of communications open. (Remember – public instruction can be perceived as public correction and your 6 year old didn't like that, so how do you think your 26 year old feels about it?)

Go light on the "honor your father and mother…" scriptures and win your son or daughter's heart with your kindness. Nothing pushes away adults faster than someone who insists on being treated a certain way.

Share your wisdom, wisely.

The Power of Speaking a Blessing

There are many good Christian books about speaking a blessing over your child. Unfortunately, when our adult children stop valuing our opinion, we may stop speaking a blessing over them.

The Harvard Business Review describes an interesting study of teams working together. Research, conducted by Emily Heaphy and Marcial Losada, examined the effectiveness of 60 leadership teams at a large information-processing company.

They found the biggest factor between the most and least successful teams was the ratio of positive comments to negative comments that the participants made to one another. Positive declarations of "I agree with that," or "That's a terrific idea," for the highest performing teams was nearly six positive comments for every one negative comment.

Negative declarations like, "I don't agree with you" or "We shouldn't even consider doing that" in the low-performing teams was a ratio of three negative comments for every one positive comment.

A Christian parent speaking a blessing is positive speech on steroids. It is not manipulative flattery or using psychology to get someone to change their behavior. Speaking a blessing has physical, emotional, mental and spiritual impact in your child's life. As the 5th commandment brings an automatic blessing upon those who honor their father and mother, so a father and mother's words create a "spiritual atmosphere" over their adult children.

Speak a blessing to them in private.
Speak a blessing to them in public settings.
Bless them with God's love.
Bless them with God's grace and mercy.
Bless them with your acceptance.

Speak a blessing each day to your kids.
Speak a blessing no matter how far from God they appear to be.
Speak a blessing with faith that God is able to save and rescue.

11

How Did My Baby Turn Out Like This?

Overcoming Confused Emotions

I first named this chapter, *"When You Don't like Your Child."* I changed it to the above title. Both are accurate when describing a very sad event that happens to many parents. There are times when it is difficult time to like an adult child. As with all adults, your child may decide to do things that are hurtful, offensive, illegal or immoral. How does a parent who loves their child and wishes them the best process their negative emotions toward.

> After the flood, Noah began to cultivate the ground, and he planted a vineyard. One day he drank some wine he had made, and he became drunk and lay naked inside his tent. Ham, the father of Canaan, saw that his father was naked and went outside and told his brothers.
>
> Then Shem and Japheth took a robe, held it over their shoulders, and backed into the tent to cover their father. As they did this, they looked the other way so they would not see him naked. *Genesis 9:20-23*

After suffering years of reproach and ridicule, Noah curses his son and grandson. The sin of not covering Noah's nakedness was a serious dishonoring of Noah. Obviously after Noah's sacrifice and obedience to God, he did not expect his adult son to treat him so sinfully. There was a valid reason for Noah to confront his son's behavior. Shem and Japheth concerned about their father gave him honor and their actions brought a blessing upon them.

How Did My Baby Turn Out Like This?

The idea that you do not like your child sounds like something that would never happen to most Christian parents. This emotion is unexpected. If and when it happens to you, your first reaction is to think what a horrible parent you are. How could you feel these feelings toward your child?

The fact that you do not like many adults for many reasons does not seem to minimize the guilt of not "loving," your child. With other adults you can withdraw from them when they change their behavior. Your internal judgments of what is right and wrong start with "loving" your child.

There may be a number of reasons why you have a problem liking your child. Being honest about your emotions and why you are having them is the first step of processing this feeling.

What Is Your Relationship

Which of these words describes your relationship with your child?

__ Close __ Good __ Uncomfortable __ Broken
__ Bad __ Guarded __ Distant __ Dreaded

Your child and you will decide how distant or how close the relationship will be. You may have little control depending upon your personality and your child's personality. But unresolved negative emotions will create a bad relationship. Your anger, fear, offense, or unforgiveness hinders your ability to react correctly when your child may change their behavior.

It takes courage to face the fact that although you love your child and are bonded to them for life, you do not like them. Parents of minor children, preteens and teens live with this dichotomy much of the time. Because the child is growing, changing and becoming a different person, parents hope for the best.

Parents hope that their minor children's instability is normal. They hope they will turn out to be good people. Even when unexpected things happen, parents hope for the best. Children need parents that believe for good things in their future and look for the best.

But now your son or daughter is 35 years old and you don't like the person they have become.

Mirroring Bad Behavior

Your child may have taken the one or two bad personality traits that you exhibited and automatically grew in them. They not only picked up your bad habits by mirroring your behavior, they have grown in your bad behavior. If you had a tendency to become angry occasionally when under a lot of stress, your son's anger may be your behavior but 10 times worse.

As a mother, if you occasionally had an emotional melt down when things became overwhelming, your daughter's emotional outbursts may be your behavior magnified 10 times.

Your child may be growing in behavior patterns that they have seen you do that are not sinful. As a father, you may have started out insecure and quietly learning from those around you. But somewhere around your 45th birthday, you became more confident and assured about life and the issues of life. Your self-assured pronouncements were based on decades of learning. Your son now mirrors your confidence but his self-assured pronouncements are based upon a YouTube video that is 5 minutes long.

Review what behavior it is that you do not like. Then objectively review if this is mirrored behavior. Is your negative emotions based on a subjective view. If you watched your neighbor's child act the way your child is acting, would you have the same response? It may be more about your reaction upon seeing your "bad-side" in your child.

How Did My Baby Turn Out Like This?

Increasing in Bad Behavior

II Samuel 13 NCV Selected verses
(King) David had a son named Absalom and a son named
Amnon. Absalom had a beautiful sister named Tamar, and
Amnon loved her. Tamar was a virgin. Amnon made himself
sick just thinking about her…. So Amnon went to bed and
acted sick.

When King David came in to see him, Amnon said to him,
"Please let my sister Tamar come in. Let her make two of her
special cakes…. Amnon said to Tamar, "Bring the food into the
bedroom so I may eat from your hand." ….. Amnon grabbed
her. He said, "Sister, come and have sexual relations with me."
Tamar said to him, "No, brother! Don't force me…

He was stronger than she was, so he forced her to have sexual
relations with him. After that, Amnon hated Tamar. He hated
her more than he had loved her before. Amnon said to her, "Get
up and leave!"… So Tamar lived in her brother Absalom's
house and was sad and lonely….

When King David heard the news, he was very angry. Absalom
did not say a word, good or bad, to Amnon. But he hated
Amnon for disgracing his sister Tamar.

The story continues with Absalom planning how to use his father, King
David, to kill Amnon. Later, Absalom takes the kingdom from his
father and is finally killed in a battle. David's adult children's bad
behavior showed their bad character. They were not nice people. They
were not good people. No matter how close David was to his minor
children. No matter how he enjoyed them, their behavior as adults was
devastating to his relationship with them.

Because honesty is one of the foundations of a good relationship, you should be honest with yourself about your child's behavior. That small fragile sweet child that you have raised may now be one of the bad people in the world, making life worse for others.

It is sobering to admit the truth that your child is not a good person. Whether their bad behavior has developed over years of self- centered choices or has come from a traumatic event, they may continue to act badly. Their behavior does affect your relationship with them.

Growing in Judging Right from Wrong

"Why is she doing that?"
"How can he do that to us?"

If you are experiencing a "King David" event in your life, confusion clouds your ability to react correctly. It is harder for you to help if you pretend that he is a good person and tomorrow he will magically act differently. There is behavior that requires repentance. There is behavior that requires restitution. There is not just bad behavior but evil behavior.

As King David's story unfolds, whether he made a lot of mistakes or only a few mistakes is not relevant to how his adult children should be judged. Once his children are doing evil things, they are responsible for their actions and how they are affecting family relationships.

We could change all the things that King David did wrong and it may or may not affect the bad behavior of his children. It is good to be self-aware and understand the mistakes you have made as a parent. But this awareness is not a part of judging current behavior. To be just in your judgments you must judge the behavior without assigning extenuating circumstances.

Setting Behavior Perimeters

You cannot control your adult child's behavior. But you can establish what behavior you will participate in. You control whether you will be in close proximity to someone who lashes out violently. You can stop giving your child access to your resources, if they cannot be trusted.

Draw a red line and stick to it. Tell your child that to have a good relationship she must stop or start doing specific behavior; then be specific. If the problem is drugs, then the red line is drawn at the possession or use of drugs. If the problem is loud angry outbursts, then draw the red line at the specific disrespectful behavior.

Establish consequences for bad behavior which are reasonable and then stick with the Red Line. Your inaction or inconsistency is understandable. Your child's bad behavior may can you intense pain. The hardest thing a parent has to do is confront a grown child with a Red Line that has the potential of breaking the relationship. God will help you develop a plan that is in your child's best interest.

The Truth Sets You Free From Deception and Confusion
Judge Behavior with Clarity

Repetitive bad behavior, month after month, will create a bad relationship, no matter what the underlying causes. There may be seasons of your child's life when the only relationship you can have with them is a bad relationship. Facing this truth will help you go forward with clarity and correct discernment.

"I have a bad relationship with my son because....
"I have a broken relationship with my daughter because she continues to ....
"I have a strained and tense relationship with my children because they keep doing ....

When relating to other adults, after a few months of bad behavior you would distance yourself from the offending party. But this is your child and it is complicated. There are other family members to consider. Your grandchildren may need your care. So go forward with your eyes wide open.

> Guard your heart above all else,
> for it determines the course of your life.
> *Proverbs 4:23 NLV*

Whatever the reason you continue in a bad relationship, you must guard your heart. Guard your mind and heart against the sourness of a continuing in a bad relationship.

The definition of mercy is to help or give someone what they don't deserve. Give mercy with the understanding that you are giving your child what they don't deserve.

> "Blessed are the merciful
> For they shall receive mercy
> *Matthew 5:7 NASB*

Most of us have needed mercy sometime in our past. We may need mercy sometime in the future. We all love to see justice and in America we are thankful we live in a culture that still values justice. But in our close relationships we all love to also receive the opposite of justice, mercy. We are glad that we are NOT getting exactly what we deserve. This is the basis of Jesus's instruction to "Turn the other cheek," in Matthew 5:38-42. You can decide to be merciful to your offending child, while setting strong boundaries of behavior.

> The way of a fool is right in his own eyes,
> But a wise man is he who listens to counsel.
> *Proverbs 12:15 NASB*

Recognizing Appropriate Behavior

Seek out seasoned, objective counsel. What is appropriate behavior of a parent to an adult child is easily blurred by what we wish would happen. People who behave badly justify their bad behavior. A Christian counselor's job is to give you a Biblical perspective that defines the appropriate and the inappropriate. Sunday morning messages may or may not apply to your situation. A good counselor can bring the wisdom that is required to apply the right truth at the right time.

Avoid the religious "one size fits all" approach. This two dimensional approach will not help with complicated problems.

Jesus confronted the merchants in the Temple at the Passover in John 2:13-16, and publicly condemned their bad behavior. Then He refused to pronounce judge upon the woman caught in the act of adultery in John 8:3-11. Ask for the wisdom of a three dimensional perspective of God's principles as you try to have the best relationship you can have.

Become a Realist

Read the proverbs each day and become a realist, full of faith and hope. Love rejoices in the truth. God is the ultimate realist. God sees everything all the time the way it really is. He sees everything exactly as it really is and was and will be. God sees the "why" of everyone's different opinions and sees all the shades of gray in human behavior.

You can view your child's bad behavior with God's understanding by mediating upon the Wisdom books of the Bible. Take a month and mediate upon Jesus' words of wisdom from the gospels. Take another month and absorb the Psalms wisdom. Become a person that loves the wisdom of the Bible.

Become a realist who has a wish list that is grounded in faith. Stop wishful thinking that hopes for a change, just because. Your child needs more than an optimist. They need someone who will take hold of the promises of God and faithfully hope in God. Hoping in people can be really disappointing. Hoping in God will be rewarding. Be a realist who has a wish list of promises for your child.

Incremental Behavior Changes

I am always looking for a giant break through. Some event that is pivotal to a change in bad behavior. I am by nature impatient. I want to see things happen, NOW.

Impatience is the opposite of faith. It does not endure. Encourage yourself to look for something to positively proclaim each day. Look for small changes in your child's behavior and positive changes in the relationship.

Approach your broken or stressed relationships with your children as areas where small changes will make a difference.

Each day keep your hope and faith in God. As you look for positive things, your faith should remain in your loving Heavenly Father. He does not change. He is with you as you look for the positive in a situation that is full of darkness.

Each day keep the faith; faith in God.

12

When Should I Help Financially?
Don't Rob Your Child of God's Lessons

In the first years of my marriage, Michelle and I lived from paycheck to paycheck. We learned to pay our rent and save money for food. We would always run out of money just as the next paycheck came. Well actually a few days before the check would come. We would order one pizza and write a check that was only good as the next check was deposited to cover it.

For the first 15 years of my marriage we did not have a credit card. A few months after we were married I lost my job. I will always remember the emotions I felt when the call came that it was going to cost $285.00 to fix the brakes on our car. We never thought to ask our parents for the money. We were happy to be on our own and took it as a badge of accomplishment that we were independent.

This chapter is written to parents who have the ability to help. If you have no extra money, then the decision has already been made for you. To all who could help, this chapter explores the complicated landscape of when, why and how we should help our children financially.

The underlying principle of when and how to help is, "Don't rob your adult children by giving them money." There are foundational lessons that God teaches all who would do right and live as responsible adults. Paul described this clearly.

> Not that I speak from want, for I have learned to be content in whatever circumstances I am. I know how to get along with humble means, and I also know how to live in prosperity; in any and every circumstance I have learned the secret of being filled and going hungry, both of having abundance and suffering need.
> *Philippians 4:11-12 NASB*

It is a Christian foundational value to learn this lesson. When learned through experience this principle removes the fear of advancing in life without full provision. It removes the fear of random events that may rob us of our resources. It teaches us faith in God. We can proceed with full confidence knowing things will be OK, because He can make them OK.

The Three Types of Financial Help

It is great when you have the resources to help your children's family when unforeseen things happen. It is great that you have extra each month. It is great that you have money set aside each month to help the poor. The Christian values of charity toward the poor; giving a portion of your income; saving a portion of your income; and managing your assets wisely can confuse the issue, when the subject of helping your adult children comes up.

There are two types of financial help. Defining the need can help you bring wisdom into your decision making. This chapter and the next chapter only begins this process of finding wisdom. In one case the decision may be obvious. The next request may become very complicated.

1. One time help for an unforeseen emergency.
2. Regular help with the expenses of life.
3. Reoccurring help that rescues your child from bad decisions.

It is a parent's joy to help their children. This joy does not stop when they leave home and become independent. It is our concern that drives us to rescue when there may not be a real need to rescue. It is our desire that our adult children experience better lives. It is our desire to shield our children from the normal pressures of life that causes us to want to rescue when we really don't need to rescue.

When Should I Help Financially?

If you are trying to shield your children from the pain of going without, you may be doing the wrong thing. There should be a balance to your help. We all want our children to grow up with as little pain as possible. But the Apostle Paul writes in Philippians 4:12, "suffering need," can be a valuable lesson. It can be a freeing lesson, as the person learns that "suffering need," is something that can be endured with a positive testimony of God's provision.

Going without a place to live is a serious need. Learning you can't spend more on your credit card than is possible to pay is a life lesson. How, when and why you are helping your adult child is determined by reviewing whether you are accomplishing your main goal of parenting.

The Goal of Helping

Your main goal is different than the goal of being a parent of a child who is dependent upon you. As a good parent of a minor child you were responsible to provide your child's needs. Shelter, clothing, food and comfort were provided each month because of your faithfulness. If you had not done this, you would have missed you goal of parenting a minor child.

Your goal now is to help your children to learn to lead happy lives that are moral, responsible and productive. Each of your actions of financial help can be judged in the light of this main parenting goal. Is my help really helping your children to be independent?

Jerry had three sons when she divorced her husband. She was 26 years old. Her mother and father tried to help as much as possible. They helped out financially most months, even though they had little extra money. By the time she was thirty Jerry was drinking every day and doing various drugs. She found a man that also liked the partying life style.

Jerry would leave her sons alone at home, for long periods of time. Her oldest son, who also became an alcoholic later in life, learned to call his grandparents when they needed something. Jerry's parents raised her three sons.

She is now 58 years old. She is homeless. Her parents are dead. She still has a drug and drinking problem. She is in the early stages of alcohol dementia. There is a chance that no one could have really helped Jerry. But it was not until her adult sons did an intervention in her mid-fifties that Jerry went into a center to get help.

Should You Help Principle #1
Don't let fear and strong emotions make you have weak love.

Jerry's mother and father had strong emotions.
Jerry's mother and father had weak love.

Jerry's parents had righteous actions toward their grandchildren. They sacrificed and gave of their time and energy to help them not just survive but to know God. In their older years, they found themselves busy doing things a younger parent should be doing.

But toward their child, their strong emotions disabled their ability to help Jerry. Who knows? If they had been strong in their love and confronted Jerry in her thirties, she might have chosen a different path. Maybe it would have taken several stays in a rehab center. If they had said, "Stop this behavior or lose your sons." Who knows?

I talked with Jerry's mother the year before she died. Jerry was living with her and had a hateful attitude toward her. Jerry was blaming her for all her problems. I encouraged her to give Jerry an ultimatum, "Change your behavior toward me or move out!" Her mother felt that would be best. When nothing had happened months later, I asked what happened to her ultimatum.

Jerry's mother had heard of another parent forcing their adult son, with a drug problem, to move out if he did not stop doing drugs. He had moved out and died from a head injury. He had simply fallen in the street. She was really scared that Jerry would die if she was forced to leave. So Jerry abused her mom until her mom's death.

When Should I Help Financially?

After all her parents help, Jerry was not thankful. Her lack of thankfulness can be viewed all through our society. Those who are supported over a long period of time, become dependent upon those who support them. Their attitude becomes the opposite of Paul's pronouncement. They do not learn to be content. Their attitudes are actually corrupted by those who are trying to help them.

Much of the time long term charity becomes an unjust action. Short term charity will help those who are in need to find a new path. Short term charity will rescue someone who has made bad decisions. But only when it is short term and someone linked to required action by those receiving help.

Should You Help Principle #2
Don't rescue your child when they are still in the pig pen

And He said, "A man had two sons. The younger of them said to his father, 'Father, give me the share of the estate that falls to me.' So he divided his wealth between them. And not many days later, the younger son gathered everything together and went on a journey into a distant country, and there he squandered his estate with loose living.

Now when he had spent everything, a severe famine occurred in that country, and he began to be impoverished. So he went and hired himself out to one of the citizens of that country, and he sent him into his fields to feed swine. And he would have gladly filled his stomach with the pods that the swine were eating, and no one was giving *anything* to him.

But when he came to his senses, he said, 'How many of my father's hired men have more than enough bread, but I am dying here with hunger! I will get up and go to my father, and will say to him, "Father, I have sinned against heaven, and in your sight; I am no longer worthy to be called your son; make me as one of your hired men." of mine was dead and has come to life again; he was lost and has been found.' And they began to celebrate. *Luke 15:11-24 NASB*

Don't be a parent that rescues your prodigal in the pig pen, before they repent or at least come to their senses. Weak love and strong emotions tempt parents to rescue with their credit card. It is repentance that will help your child overcome and not repeat the behavior that lead to the pig pen. Don't rob your child of a lesson that could influence future directions of his life.

Should You Help Principle #3
Speak the Truth When Helping

Speaking the truth in love,
we are to grow up in all aspects
into Him who is the head, even Christ,
Ephesians 4:15

We are not just to love but to speak the truth in love. When you are asked for help, you should speak the truth. The opportunities for your adult child to "hear" the truth from you may be limited. You may have only a few opportunities to speak into your child's life in the areas of their failure. And if they need to be regularly rescued they are failing.

Most adults do not like unsolicited advice. In religious circles there is always someone who either out of concern or just unperceived arrogance feels the need to share their opinion on where we are going wrong. Self-appointed "Sin Detectors" can be quite annoying.

But you are your child's parent. It is a good practice for you to wait to be asked for your opinion. But in this case you are being asked for help. You want to see growth, as described in Ephesian 4:15. Speak the truth in love. Be kind. Be gentle. But be honest.

They may not want to hear. They may not be open to what you have to say. Quietly ask simple open questions. "Why do you think this happened? What could or should happen so this won't happen next year?"

When Should I Help Financially?

Talking to an Adult Child Is an Art

We learn to talk to adults differently, depending upon the relationship. You know how to talk to your boss, your pastor, your friends, and your spouse. But parents learn to avoid talking with their children about sensitive issues. And there is nothing as sensitive as your children asking you for help.

I have addressed in other chapters when to hold your piece. But when your child comes to you for regular help, do not avoid speaking into their lives. This is the one time that your love for your child mandates your speaking.

Take a big breathe. Talk quietly. Talk slowly. But talk.

Should You Help Principle #4
Just the Facts – Define the Problem

Before you decide if you should help, define the problem. Not the problem that your child has brought to you, but the cause of the problem. Find the answer to a few questions that will help you define the problem.

1. What type of request? One time; regular; reoccurring rescue?
2. Is this outside of your child's control?
3. If you help, will you be putting the problem off a few months, only to see it return?
4. What is the RIGHT thing that you should do?

Principle #5
Do What Is Right

In real life problems there may be five RIGHT things to do and ten WRONG things. Defining not just the problem and how to address the issues surrounding the problem is not enough. Define what the right things to do might be. When solving problems, there are subjective questions that may be slightly different for each family and for each individual.

There is also Biblical Objective truth that can be applied similarly to every family on Earth. There are rules that are always right. There are things that are always wrong. God starts with the Ten Commandments and continues telling all of us what is right and wrong. This structure of right and wrong is true for everyone.

All of us need help judging right behavior. When it comes to the area of when and how to help without hurting, having an objective voice, is invaluable. We all have a partial understanding of Biblical Righteousness. Finding another kind and honest voice about the complicated financial matters in this chapter can help immensely.

Here are a few guidelines when looking for someone with wise input.

1. Look for someone who can state the Biblical position on moral issues. Ask for Chapter and verse and pray for wisdom.

2. Look for someone who is courageous and follow Biblical truth and speak it, clearly. Many leaders of churches will not speak the truth if it looks as if you will be offended by it.

3. Look for someone who is experienced enough to have wisdom with the application of moral principles when several issues of right and wrong collide in real life situations.

4. Look for someone who has a four dimensional approach. Many Christians have a two dimensional view of truth. They can repeat Sunday morning "sound bites" but have no understanding of the varying applications of Bible truth.

13

When Should I Help Them Leave?
And Other Ways We "Help"

Well, he came from college just the other day
So much like a man I just had to say
"Son, I'm proud of you, can you sit for a while"
He shook his head and said with a smile
"What I'd really like, Dad, is to borrow the car keys
See you later, can I have them please"

And the cat's in the cradle and the silver spoon
Little boy blue and the man on the moon
When you comin' home son
I don't know when, but we'll get together then, Dad
You know we'll have a good time then

I've long since retired, my son's moved away
I called him up just the other day
I said, "I'd like to see you if you don't mind"
He said, "I'd love to, Dad, if I can find the time
You see my new job's a hassle and kids have the flu
But it's sure nice talking to you, Dad
It's been sure nice talking to you"

And as I hung up the phone it occurred to me
He'd grown up just like me
My boy was just like me
The last verses of Cat's in the Cradle

According to Wikipedia the ***Cat's in the Cradle*** song's lyrics, by Harry Chapin, first began as a poem written by Harry's wife. The poem itself was inspired by the awkward relationship between her first husband, and his father, a New York City politician. Harry also said the song was about his own relationship with his son, Josh, admitting, "Frankly, this song scares me to death."

Midlife is the time when most of us have more responsibility, more influence and more demands upon our time. As our children leave home, our time is filled with many things that are important. Finally, when all the kids leave home, husbands and wives have time to become a couple again. Instead of juggling schedules between the kid's needs, their marriage relationship becomes the first priority.

The kids do not need them the way they use to, so it is no surprise that many parents lower the priority of "being there" for their adult children. After years of their life revolving around school, sports and music lessons, the urgency to be available for adult children disappears. They're grown up now. They can handle it.

Responsible people control their schedules to accomplish their mission in life. Or at least they try to control their schedules. This song's lyric forces all of us to review what we do with the priorities of our time.

Never Too Busy To Talk

"Never too busy to talk," can become your new parenting mandate. There were times that you had to work and not attend the 5th grade afternoon play. There were times when your kids were at home, when you balanced one thing against the importance of another. But now that they are in the "busy" season of life of their lives, it is more important that you rearrange your schedule to be there when needed.

Now that you are more in control of your time and schedule, you can be available in the area of fellowship, conversation or prayer. Your adult children may still have to make an appointment with you to get together, physically depending upon your responsibilities. But allow them to interrupt you. This change of priorities is reasonable but such a shift from former norms that it can be overlooked.

When Should I Help Them Leave?

There is a natural tendency to not respond to your adult children's requests, since they do not really need your help. And it might be true that they really don't "need" you. But you now need to stay connected to them. If you want your opinion to be respected, respond quickly in the times that they reach out to communicate.

There are practical steps a parent can take to share their newly disconnected adult child's life. Think through the practical steps you might take to make your children and grandchildren the top commitment in your scheduling. Either over the phone, when you are out of town, or sitting in a coffee shop for an hour; requests to talk can be immediately put at the top of your "to do" list.

Most friends and family members drop everything in times of emergency, to help. They rush to the hospital. What sets a parent a part from the other friends and family is their ability to drop everything, When there is NOT an emergency.

Commit to this new and different role. Drop everything to just listen. Drop everything to help with a problem. Make it your goal to always be available and accessible to my children, when they ask.

When They Haven't Fully Left

When you should and shouldn't help your adult child is one of the most complicated questions that any parent wrestles with. The last chapter was focused upon helping financially. But there are many other ways that we remain connected to those who have not fully become independent. From a room in the basement to paying for their cell phone, we continue to help our adult children.

From the time your child goes to kindergarten to helping them buy their first car, there are varying opinions of when it is appropriate to help. I can still remember the heavy Kindergarten door that I could not open at 5 years old. But my mother let me go each day without helping me. By the time I graduated to first grade, I had mastered the heavy door. My mother resisted the urge to help. And now I am glad.

Maybe you can remember the helplessness you felt as you waved goodbye to your first child on the first day of school. As the kids get older, it becomes easier and easier to NOT help.

The Myth of the Eagle and Their Young

Does the eagle really push it's young out of the nest?

People claim that the only species of bird to practice pushing their young out of the nest is the eagle, but according to studies, Ornithologists have observed eagles coaxing, even taunting, their young from the nest, rather than just giving them a shove.

When the fledgling eagle is almost ready to fly, eagle parents have been observed to swoop by the nest with a fresh kill. Instead of landing in the nest as usual to share the meal, the parent lands near the nest and eats in plain view of the hungry teenage eagle. This behavior continues until the fledgling is hungry enough to venture out of the nest, at which point the parent will share its food.

This is backed up by a discussion by Eagle Expert Peter Nye:
"No! The adults may withhold food as the eaglets get near fledging, and encourage them to fly to a nearby perch to get their meal, but that's about it. Usually, no coaxing is necessary and the eaglets are all too anxious to test their wings!"
This intentional action of not helping is as important as being there, when you have an "Eaglet" that is having trouble leaving the nest.

The Baby Races

My wife and her friends use to be in a contest with their babies. Walking, eating, potty training was talked about at the same level as an NBA championship race. Who was ahead of whom? The exact age little Johnny had stumbled across the room by himself became an area of pride. We celebrated their first steps (with and without our help.) We celebrated their feeding themselves (even when most of the food did not get into their mouths.)

When Should I Help Them Leave?

Later the whole family celebrated our children's successes.
We celebrated the Cheerleading victories.
We celebrated the elementary school plays.
We celebrated the Junior High band recitals.

Two dynamics remain in tension throughout our children's lives. We provide support, correction, instruction, food and shelter. And in tension with this provision, we encourage their independence. So that one day they will not need our support, correction, instruction, food and shelter.

Now they are in their twenties, and they look and act like adults but remain dependent. Should you push them out of the nest? Should you continue helping? Or like the eagle, should you change YOUR behavior?

Here is a list of things you might do to help your young adult eaglet leave the nest. Some are obvious. Be creative.

1. Stop buying them stuff. Sit down and talk about how you plan on proceeding. They will receive Christmas presents with the rest of the family. You will not be buying them clothes, deodorant or shampoo.

2. Stop buying their favorite foods. Buy the foods you plan on eating. That's all.

3. Stop cooking them meals. If you love to cook for your family and everyone is gone except little 30 years old Johnny, stop. Cook for yourself. Cook at the holidays for your family.

4. Stop washing, ironing or hanging their clothes up in their closet. If they are 26 years old, (or 22 - you make the cut off age – and there should be a cut off age) you are robbing your child of a valuable lesson of life.

5. Don't pay for their internet, cell phone or cable TV bills. This has been used to motivate thousands of young adults to find a job.

6. Discuss with them there plans. And there should be some type of plan.

7. If there is mental disability, physical disabilities, or emotional disabilities, find help from an objective professional. You are not going to be around forever and it is time to face the fact that your child can not live on their own. They need help and so do you.

8. Make a deadline when you will discuss a plan again. Then stick to the deadline; three months to decide and one month to move out

9. Stop making their car payments or their car insurance payments.

10. Offer to help with the costs of education with a firm date that you will stop helping.

Parents want to have a good relationship with their children. But creating a dependent relationship usually has the opposite effect upon adults. In the same way that people who are on public assistance become resentful of the agency that is supporting them, so young adults begin to be ungrateful toward parents that keep them dependent past the appropriate age.

Reasons We Make It Harder To Leave

A. We enjoy doing things for them, even when we probably shouldn't.

B. We want to remain their friend or be loved. This borders manipulation and control. It usually back fires.

C. We do want to control them and the easiest way is to keep them close.

D. We are fearful about how they will survive in the big bad world. This may be a new feeling or it may have started while they were younger. They will fail and they will succeed. Your trust must be in God and not your child.

E. You need to be a mom. You have always been loving and nurturing.

F. You prefer the company of your child over your spouse.

When Should I Help Them Leave?

If you find yourself taking your 24 year old son out to buy him tennis shoes, take a look in the mirror. Be honest with yourself. Why are you acting inappropriately and making it easier for your child to remain dependent? They may stay around, but in most cases they will love you later in their life, when you do what is right now.

Do not be an enabler but be a good parent and act like the Eagle. Don't just kick them out on the street. Create an environment where it is really, really attractive to move out.

You do not have to make a LOUD Announcement, "We are doing this to get you to finally be independent." Like the eagle it is better that you make it self-serving for them to become independent. Help your child fly - alone. He or she will be grateful to you years later, once they are comfortable on their own.

When You Are Wealthy

Boston College's Center on Wealth and Philanthropy has developed a study titled *"The Joys and Dilemmas of Wealth"* which was funded by The John Templeton Foundation and The Gates Foundation. This study is the result of a survey of 165 wealthy households. The average net worth per household surveyed was $78 million with 120 exceeding $25 million.

For the first time, researchers prompted the very rich to speak candidly about their lives. The result is a surprising litany of anxieties: their sense of isolation, their worries about work and love, and most of all, their fears for their children.

This might be the reason some of the richest men and women in the world have decided to accept Bill Gates challenge to give away 50% of their money. Here is summary from Yahoo Finance.

Bill Gates is one of the richest people in the world. But he and his wife Melinda aren't interested in keeping their money for themselves, or for their three children. "I knew I didn't think it was a good idea to give the money to my kids. That it wouldn't be good either for my kids or society," He told *The Sun* in 2010.

Instead, the Bill and Melinda Foundation has invited other wealthy individuals to join the Gates' lead and donate half their money to charity.

Warren Buffett of Berkshire Hathaway fame pledged to give away 99% of his wealth. Buffett said "I want to give my kids just enough so that they would feel that they could do anything, but not so much that they would feel like doing nothing."

Home Depot co-founder Bernard Marcus, not wanting his kids to inherit large sums of money — for their own good, he told *Forbes*, Marcus plans on giving the majority of his Home Depot stock to his foundation, which benefits the handicapped and education.

British Chef Nigella Lawson is a best-selling author and TV personality. Though Lawson herself comes from a wealthy background, she seems to be a firm believer in not giving her two children that same advantage. She came under fire for saying, "I am determined that my children should have no financial security. It ruins people not having to earn money."

Think Before You Rescue

As parents we are hardwired to rescue our children from their stupid mistakes. We have done it throughout their lives and it is only natural to continue the same behavior, when we are able. We have a good habit of making everything better. But with adult children, really making things better may require us to stop helping.

We want to take away the consequences of their actions, and relieve them and ourselves from the suffering. Making everything better may require us to do the opposite of the habit we have developed over the years. We may need to do nothing.

As the Eagle allows some discomfort to motivate their young, so we should look for and allow discomfort to bring maturity in our children's lives. As problems develop we can react one of three ways.

When Should I Help Them Leave?

Reaction 1
Be an Encourager

Encouragement gives your child strength to continue. Do you want your child to continue in the present circumstances or stop and change direction? If the problem is one that just needs to be overcome, this is the best reaction. Be positive and encourage your child that they have what it takes to overcome the set back.

Reaction 2
Be a Corrector

Confrontation and correction can help your child change their behavior or thinking about their present path. It can discourage him to NOT continue down the path that is causing the problem. Confrontation can produce repentance. Is repentance needed in this situation?

Reaction 3
Do Nothing

There are times that you need to not have an opinion. There are situations that arise that your child needs to find the answer on their own. The intentional action of not having the answer makes room for your child to develop their problem solving skills. A skill that is invaluable throughout life.

Jim came to me after Sunday Morning Service deeply troubled. His daughter was in jail and being charged with assaulting someone. Should he help her? She had a small child and she and her husband had been struggling with drug problems. What should he do?

I did not give Jim an answer that day. I told Jim I would be by his side while he was going through this, but he would have to decide for himself. As a pastor, there are many times that I wish I could give a quick answer that would take away the pain and dread in the situation. But there were too many variables to make the decision for Jim.

Was his daughter willing to go to rehab?
Who would provide care for the baby?
Could he get the money to bail her out of jail?
Would her removal from jail be better for her?
Did Jim and his wife have the emotional stamina to keep their daughter in jail?

We prayed. He ended up rescuing her from the situation only to have her mental illness bring them to a place that they had to take legal custody of their granddaughter. Did he make the right decision? Only time will tell what was the best action.

There may be times that your Eaglets should be rescued from falling to their death and there are other times that you should begin a systematic process of enticing your Eaglets to leave the nest and fly.

It is easy for those around you and especially well-intentioned church friends to take a hard line for actions in one direction or another. Rescue or do not rescue? One friend exhorts you to rescue and the other brings up the misunderstood eagle story. They pronounce with certainty, "Push them out of the nest."

As one of the final parental decisions that you make, you will have to decide. Your child gaining their independence will probably take longer than you think it will. So decide to fight the good fight and finish the course. Your kids have almost grown up and they need you to be an adult, whether they think they do or not.

Cat's In the Cradle
My child arrived just the other day
He came to the world in the usual way
But there were planes to catch and bills to pay
He learned to walk while I was away
And he was talkin' 'fore I knew it, and as he grew
He'd say "I'm gonna be like you, Dad
You know I'm gonna be like you"

When Should I Help Them Leave?

And the cat's in the cradle and the silver spoon
Little boy blue and the man on the moon
When you comin' home, Dad
I don't know when, but we'll get together then
You know we'll have a good time then

My son turned ten just the other day
He said, "Thanks for the ball, Dad, come on let's play
can you teach me to throw", I said "Not today
I got a lot to do", he said, "That's ok
And he walked away but his smile never dimmed
And said, "I'm gonna be like him, yeah
You know I'm gonna be like him"

And the cat's in the cradle and the silver spoon
Little boy blue and the man on the moon
When you comin' home, Dad
I don't know when, but we'll get together then
You know we'll have a good time then

Well, he came from college just the other day
So much like a man I just had to say
"Son, I'm proud of you, can you sit for a while"
He shook his head and said with a smile
"What I'd really like, Dad, is to borrow the car keys
See you later, can I have them please"

And the cat's in the cradle and the silver spoon
Little boy blue and the man on the moon
When you comin' home son
I don't know when, but we'll get together then, Dad
You know we'll have a good time then

I've long since retired, my son's moved away
I called him up just the other day
I said, "I'd like to see you if you don't mind"
He said, "I'd love to, Dad, if I can find the time
You see my new job's a hassle and kids have the flu
But it's sure nice talking to you, Dad
It's been sure nice talking to you"

And as I hung up the phone it occurred to me
He'd grown up just like me
My boy was just like me

And the cat's in the cradle and the silver spoon
Little boy blue and the man in the moon
When you comin' home son
I don't know when, but we'll get together then, Dad
We're gonna have a good time then

14

What Do I Do Now That They Are Gone?

Enjoying the Final Seasons of Your Life

The fruit of the Spirit is love, joy, peace
Galatians 5:22a NASB

Most humans want what God has promised all His children. They seek some combination of love, joy and peace; sometimes mixed with security, comfort or stimulation.

How do we experience love, joy and peace in the final seasons of our life? With so many changes, many of us have real challenges living a positive and balanced lifestyle.

We have all been encouraged to work toward the time of retirement as something that is going to be great. We are told that in retirement, if we plan, work hard, save and have a little luck, it will be great. We don't have to work. We don't have to produce anymore. We won't have any pressures. We won't be carrying a lot of responsibility.

This 20th Century definition of the American Dream of retirement is an illusion. This is a perversion of the American Dream. The true American Dream is that we can have the freedom to pursue good things; the freedom to accomplish great things; and the freedom to build a better world for our children and other people's children. Early retirement is a Baby Boomer dream and it does not work.

Only the lazy look forward to doing nothing. You and I have something to do that is valuable. We have something to do that will impact those around us. We are called to end our lives well.

No One Needs You

Karl called one day and said, "I have a lot to do today. I have been gone several weeks and have a stack of mail 2 feet high to dig through." I knew that the stack of mail was mainly junk mail and suspected something that Karl was unaware of. Karl needed a job. He needed a job to feel better about life. He had given himself a job of processing junk mail.

Karl was one of the healthiest men I had known. He was active and always doing something. He had a great job with a great retirement plan. He retired in his middle 50's and lived into his 80's. For the last 25 years of Karl's life, he had no responsibility, no accomplishments and no job. He thought he was living "The Good Life."

Karl liked to say, "You know I am on a fixed income now." For more than 25 years, he was on a really, really good fixed income, with health insurance fully paid for until he died. There was no monetary reason for him to accomplish anything.

Karl had been deceived by the 21st Century American Dream of working hard so you don't have to work. This deception had robbed him of one quarter of his life's work.

Karl was not living the American Dream. He was living a self-centered dream. Once he retired, he had the opportunity to make a difference in any area of the world that he chose. Since happiness comes from finding a path of accomplishment, Karl had also been robbed of true happiness.

Discipline Yourself to Keep Your Appointments

You may not have to be anywhere at a specific time, now that you have control of your schedule. You may not have any appointments for the next month. But you have a daily, a weekly and several annual appointments with a very important person. These three appointments describe the rhythms of God's love relationship with you. The three appointments are:

What Do I Do Now That They Are Gone?

Your Daily Manna Appointment

God has an appointment with you each day. He will be there. Will You? Each day there is a special time of connection between you and God. But you can miss your appointments, by just not committing to a daily time with God. You may not have a commitment to a job today. But you can still live a disciplined lifestyle. Each day you can walk with God by simply setting aside a time to meet with him.

This time is not a religious time of dreaded duty, but a time of special relationship. You may not feel like doing it every day, but once you establish a new habit of gathering fresh manna every day, you will never go back to eating that wormy, stall stuff from yesterday.

Each of the appointments God has waiting for you to come and meet with him are times of Him sharing himself with you. You only have to come. God had a daily time of communion with Adam in the Garden and still desires this time with all His children. Most don't show up. They have more important things to do.

Your Weekly Appointment

I always wondered why the commandment of the Sabbath day is included as one of the ten most important moral laws of God. It would seem to me that there are other things that could have been included as more important to the establishment of good and evil behavior. I missed the "Why" of the Sabbath, when looking at it as a hard, forced, grit your teeth duty to God. "Keep it Holy" had little meaning to my western mind.

But as my life unfolded, I began to perceive the importance of this setting a time aside for God each week. It wasn't just getting away from my daily work, although that helped me work harder the other 6 days. I began to perceive that the other 6 days went better, when I took time with my God Relationship on the seventh.

Now I make sure I keep my weekly date with God. Sometimes I feel dull and unexcited. But recently I really look forward to our meetings. It is a part of God's love relationship with humanity. Somehow and this really is a mystery to me, God loves my company. He waits for me to come to HIS APPOINTMENTS.

To Work or Not to Work
Stay Positive

Now that you are retired, take a few years and try new things. Like Karl, you may have 25 years to accomplish great things. A person can accomplish a lot in two decades, even going half speed. Take a few years and find your new "job." God has work for you that He wants to do with you. You can be more successful than you were in the other seasons.

No one wants to be around grandpa when he is always negative and grouchy. He complains about life and the changing world with a hopeless attitude that comes from his disappointment of life after work. His adult children may be at their wits end as they try to help grandpa do what only grandpa can do. Start living again. Older age has a lot of physical challenges. But it is forced inactivity that really slows us down.

Develop a schedule that fits your lifestyle that includes learning, working and some entertainment. Exercise your body, soul and spirit each week with a schedule that is no longer dictated by your young children's needs. God has a schedule for you that is full of good things.

If this sounds like a lot of work or a lot of time learning new things, it is. And that is the one thing you have, time. You are now living in a season when time really matters. Make your time count. Learning new things keeps your mind alert and your emotions level.

Find your area of passion and become an expert. Find your interests and then leave your comfort zone. Finding your passion is not finding the place that you are the most comfortable with but the place that you can expand and stretch the most.

What Do I Do Now That They Are Gone?

Do the Work of a Grandparent
Be Available When You Don't Want To Be

Chapter 5 explores the work of a Grandparent. Set a goal that when you are able, you will help those who ask for your help. This season of life should give you more flexibility to be available. You may have more time to respond to life's problems than when life was so busy. You may be the one who safe guards your grandkids just by being there when others can't.

Be a Part of History

And there was a man in Jerusalem whose name was Simeon; and this man was righteous and devout, looking for the consolation of Israel; and the Holy Spirit was upon him. And it had been revealed to him by the Holy Spirit that he would not see death before he had seen the Lord's Christ.

And he came in the Spirit into the temple; and when the parents brought in the child Jesus, to carry out for Him the custom of the Law, then he took Him into his arms, and blessed God, and said,

"Now Lord, You are releasing
Your bond-servant to depart in peace,
According to Your word;
For my eyes have seen Your salvation,
Which You have prepared in the presence of all peoples,
A Light of revelation to the Gentiles,
And the glory of Your people Israel."

And His father and mother were amazed at the things which were being said about Him. And Simeon blessed them and said to Mary His mother, "Behold, this Child is appointed for the fall and rise of many in Israel, and for a sign to be opposed—and a sword will pierce even your own soul—to the end that thoughts from many hearts may be revealed."

And there was a prophetess, Anna the daughter of Phanuel, of the tribe of Asher. She was advanced in years and had lived with her husband seven years after her marriage, and then as a widow to the age of eighty-four. She never left the temple, serving night and day with fastings and prayers. At that very moment she came up and began giving thanks to God, and continued to speak of Him to all those who were looking for the redemption of Jerusalem. *Luke 2:5-38 NASB*

Our generation is projected to live longer and be healthier than any generation in history. This is the time for the Simeons and the Annas. While the world discounts the impact of those over 60, God is giving you an invitation to be a part of His story in this generation. You can make a difference. Your energy may not be what it used to be. But you can have the testimony of David. Start now at walking with God and end with David's testimony.

A Psalm of David
The steps of a man are established by the Lord,
And He delights in his way.
When he falls, he will not be hurled headlong,
Because the Lord is the One who holds his hand.

I have been young and now I am old,
Yet I have not seen the righteous forsaken
Or his descendants begging bread.
All day long he is gracious and lends,
And his descendants are a blessing.
Psalm 37:23-26 NASB

A Final Word

It is hard to define what the best relationship is between parents and their adult children. When they are living in the home, most of us could grade each of the relationships on a scale of one to ten; ten being best. That is why throughout this book, I have used the phrase, "have as good of a relationship as you can have with your adult child." This was the working title of this book, but it was a bit too long and clumsy for publication.

There is a natural process of learning, in which we compare things to see what works and what doesn't. This natural process breaks down when we compare our relationships with other families. Each family has so many different dynamics that to compare is foolish.

We see the much too public estrangement of Lachlan Murdoch from his Billionaire father, Rupert Murdoch, the builder of News Corp. We hear how they no longer speak and how Rupert had such high hopes for his son, only to be rebuffed. We wonder how much is true and how much is a competitor's embellishment.

We read in Forbes Magazine about H. Ross Perot Jr. the 54-year-old son of billionaire H. Ross Perot Sr. How he continued in his father's footsteps and made the third billion of his family's fortune developing an inland transportation center near Fort Worth Texas. One generation building upon the success of the last, without dishonoring "leaks" to the press.

We see pictures of Mitt Romney's family reunions at Lake Winnipesaukee in Wolfeboro, N.H. Where his 18 grandchildren participate in a talent show, and they all live happily ever after. They probably have relationship problems, but they seem so happy. In the Romney's case, if there was dirt about family discord, it would have surfaced in 2012. Intergenerational relationships seem to be important to the whole family. Good for them.

God's Help for Parents with Adult Children

When I started writing the skeleton of this book, I had an average grade of maybe 7 or 8 when grading all four of my adult children's relationship to their mother and me. In our case a disruptive influence was introduced half way through the writing of this book, and several of the chapters were modified as I experienced first-hand the deep pain of a dishonoring child.

Now I have as good of a relationship that a parent could have with one of my children. I am respected. I am honored and we enjoy just hanging out together. But I also have one of the worse relationships that a person could have with their adult child. The joy of the first can never negate the pain of the second. I assume that most of us live with this mixture of the good, bad and ugly relationships. For those of us who are perfectionists or control-freaks, the pain is probably greater.

This book was a labor of love for my fellow parents who worked hard, sacrificed much and still are challenged with seeming insurmountable problems in their families.

We live in a time that we can take great comfort in the last verses of the Book of Job. After the trauma that Job went through, here is his final testimony.

> In all the land were found no women so beautiful as the daughters of Job; and their father gave them an inheritance among their brothers.

> After this Job lived one hundred and forty years, and saw his children and grandchildren for four generations. So Job died, old and full of days. *Job 42:15-17 NKJV*

I would ask you to set a high goal for your relationship with your children and your grandchildren. Although I am not there yet, I will work toward this high goal with you. Learning from my mistakes and weathering the storm, we can finish well.

May God bless you. May we have the best relationship that we can have with our adult children.

A Letter to My Kids
Now That You Are Adults

Whenever you are hurting, I hurt too.
Whenever you are happy, I am happy too.
Whenever you succeed, I rejoice with your success.
Whenever you fail, I am there with you too.

When you were small, there were times that it appeared that this was not true.
A good parent sometimes must put their child's character development before their child's wishes and happiness.
So, when you were small, it may have seemed that I did not care about your struggles or successes, as much as the rightness of your actions.

But now that you are older, and my work of molding you into a responsible good person is mostly done, let me share something that you may already know, since you are now an adult.

When you struggled with fear as a child, I struggled with you.
When you had a bad day with your friends, I hurt with you.
When you won a contest or did well on a test, I rejoiced with you.

Although your happiness was never my primary objective as a parent, your unhappiness always affected me. When someone you love suffers, what can you do but feel their pain.

As a parent it was my job not just to mold your character.
It was also my job to hide things from you.
I hid the times we did not have money to buy food.
I hid the times we struggled with not having a job and relocating.
I hid the times when your mother and my relationship had serious problems.

APPENDIX I

It is not a parent's job to share adult pressures and struggles with their children. Life is hard enough in fourth grade. In grade school, you did not need the complications from the messed up adult world that parents live in.

As a teenager, you began to become aware of the imperfections of life and your parents. You began to notice when I did not say the right thing or I was self-absorbed with a personal problem and not engaged with your feelings.

When you were a teenager, life got a lot harder for me and you. But even then, you were sheltered from 90% of the adult things happening in my life.
As a teenager it seemed even more evident that your happiness was not my primary goal. You may have missed this fact. When you were happy, I was happy.

Now you are an adult and I hope that in the future there will be times that we can share things as adults.

Now that you are older, and I no longer have to be the one who holds things together. I just wanted you to know.

When you hurt, I hurt.
When you succeed, I rejoice.
When you stumble, I want to jump to help.
When you fail, I am there with you too.

I have always loved you.

DAD

I mailed this letter to all four of my children a few years ago, to express my love.

About the Author

GREGORY B GRINSTEAD was senior pastor of Palmdale Christian Fellowship, a church in Southern California for over 25 years.

Gregory and his wife Michelle have four adult children and are currently living in the Kansas City area. They minister in churches throughout the United States.

Gregory is also the author of the following books.

The Hidden Promise
How to Honor Your Parents

Is God a Capitalist?
A Guide to 21st Century Questions

You can email the author at Greg@Zone7.tv

Made in the USA
Middletown, DE
08 January 2017